One Hundred Things to do at Walt Disney World Before You Die

The Ultimate Bucket List — Magic Kingdom, Epcot, Disney Animal Kingdom, and Disney Hollywood Studios Edition

CATHERINE F. OLEN

One Hundred Things to do at Walt Disney World Before you Die
The Ultimate Bucket List – Magic Kingdom, Epcot, Disney Animal Kingdom, and Disney Hollywood Studios Edition

© 2020 Catherine Olen

All Rights Reserved. No portion of this book may be reproduced, stored in a retrieval system, or transmitted in any form or by any means – electronic, mechanical, photocopy, recording, scanning or other – except for brief quotations in critical reviews or articles, without the prior written permission of the publisher. Subject to permission under section 107 and/or 108 of the 1976 United States Copyright act. Requests for permission should be addressed to the publisher www.mousehangover.com. 949-234-7332

First paperback edition June 2020
ISBN 978-1-64822-008-1 (paperback)
ISBN 978-1-64822-009-8 (eBook)

Published by Mouse Hangover
www.Mousehangover.com

Please note: Every effort has been made to ensure the accuracy of information throughout this book. The information is believed to be accurate at the time of printing. The publish and author are not responsible for errors or omissions, for changes to details or the consequences of the readers reliance to the information provided. Attraction closures or updates are not the responsibility of the publisher or author and cannot be guaranteed at the time of use of this book.

Readers are welcome to contact the publisher for comments, updates or questions.

About the Author

Catherine Olen has been visiting Disney parks since she was a small child. Olen fell in love with the parks built through the imagination of Walt Disney and became an annual passholder in 1991 and has held an annual pass ever since.

Olen first traveled to Walt Disney World at the age of thirty, immediately falling in love with the Florida parks. She has traveled to the Walt Disney World theme parks each year since and now travels to Orlando several times a year to revel in the new attractions as well as the classic favorites.

Olen now shares her love of all things Disney in *The Great Walt Disney World Scavenger Hunt*.

Come Check Us Out

Check out new books, video and news at
www.Mousehangover.com
Subscribe to Mouse Hangover
Instagram - @TheMouseHangover
Twitter - @Mousehangover
Facebook - @Mousehangover
@WDWScavengerHunt

Youtube – Mouse Hangover

Other books:

The Great Disneyland Scavenger Hunt
The Great Universal Studios Hollywood Scavenger Hunt
The Great Universal Orlando Scavenger Hunt

Dedication

To everyone who gave me their support and assistance in the process of finishing this book

To every person that has fallen in love with Walt Disney World resort

Lastly, my thanks to Walt Disney for the vision that created Walt Disney World and all of the cast members who have made this adventure a magical experience.

Legal

All of the questions found in this book have been verified by several Disney enthusiasts and I am aware that the décor of Walt Disney World changes regularly. If there are changes, you can visit www.MouseHangover.com for current updates. If you have come across a change prior to finding the update on my website, please email me so the changes can be noted.

I hope you find your way through the Walt Disney World resort with new eyes and enjoy your hunt for the loving details Walt Disney wanted his guests to experience.

Note: All content is subject to change without notice. Ride closures, construction, or overlays for the Halloween and Christmas holidays may alter the content temporarily due to park-wide decorations.

Trademarks:

This book contains Disney copy-righted characters, registered trademarks, marks, and registered marks of The Walt Disney Company and Disney Enterprises Inc.

All references to these properties, and The Twilight Zone®, a registered trademark of CBS, Inc., are made solely for editorial purposes. Neither the author nor the publisher makes any commercial claim to their use, and neither is affiliated with The Walt Disney Company or CBS in any way.

All references to the properties of Aerosmith, Indiana Jones, Avatar, Star Wars and any second party characters of films are made solely for editorial purposes. Neither the author nor the publisher makes any commercial claims to their use and neither is affiliated to these works or the producing entities.

Table of Contents

Introduction xi
Before you enter the theme parks 1

Magic Kingdom 8
   Main Street U.S.A. 9
   Fantasyland 28
   Liberty Square 45
   Frontierland 55
   Adventureland 64
   Tomorrowland 72

Epcot 77
   Introduction 78
   Future World East 79
   Future World West 83
   World Showcase 89
      Mexico 90
      Norway 92
      China 95
      Germany 98
      Italy 101
      The American Adventure 102
      Japan 105
      Morocco 107
      France 109
      United Kingdom 113

  Canada 115
  Epcot Flower and Garden Festival 117
  Epcot International Food and Wine Festival 118

Disney's Animal Kingdom 121
  Introduction 122
  Discovery Island 123
  Pandora – The World of Avatar 127
  Africa 133
  Asia 137
  Dinoland U.S.A. 141

Disney's Hollywood Studio 146
  Introduction 147
  Hollywood Blvd 149
  Sunset Blvd 153
  Animation Courtyard 158
  Toy Story Land 162
  Star Wars: Galaxy's Edge 167
  Echo Lake 185
  Commissary Lane 191
  Grand Avenue 193

Holidays at Walt Disney World 198
  Halloween 199
  Magic Kingdom 200
  Disney's Hollywood Studios 203

Christmas 204
  Magic Kingdom 205
  Epcot 207
  Disney Animal Kingdom 208
  Disney's Hollywood Studios 209

Introduction

From the grand opening on October 1, 1971, Walt Disney World has held the public captive with the way founder Walt Disney brought the fairy tale world of his films to life within the gates of his theme park. Children revel in the majesty of Cinderella Castle, and adults become kids again as they cross over into Fantasyland for the first time.

Disney came to central Florida and found the perfect place to expand on his dream to create a world of his own. While Disney never lives to see his dream realized, the dream still lives with each guest that enters the gates of the Magic Kingdom, Epcot, Disney Hollywood Studios and the Disney Animal Kingdom.

If this is your first time experiencing everything that Walt Disney World has to offer, this book may help you decide what speaks to your heart. If this is your five-hundredth time walking through the gates, you may find something new to bring back some of the feelings you experienced the first time you came to this happy place.

Whether it is meeting Mickey Mouse or riding Space Mountain, there are hundreds of ways to make a to visit

Catherine F. Olen

Walt Disney World special. Flying over London with Peter Pan, traveling the ice-covered peak of Expedition Everest, soaring over the wonders of the world, or riding over the floating mountains of Pandora, you will not want to miss one moment of the excitement that awaits you.

While it is impossible to do everything at Walt Disney World in one visit, I can ensure you will not miss any of the magic when you have *One Hundred Thing to do at Walt Disney World Before you Die* as your companion on your visit.

Before you enter the theme parks

With all the excitement of a trip to Walt Disney World, it is hard to believe you would have a list outside the theme parks; however, there are several things you will want to experience throughout the resort.

While the guest's first thoughts of the Walt Disney World resort are the wonders that lay beyond the front gates of the theme parks, Disney has included many surprises throughout the resort.

☐   Ride the Monorail

   The monorail is one of the wonders of transportation inside the Walt Disney World resort. Whether you are traveling from the transportation center of the Magic Kingdom, moving from the various resorts, or visiting the theme parks of the Magic Kingdom and Epcot, the monorail offers a bird's eye view of the resort around you.

The air-conditioned cars allow guests to travel in comfort while they whisk you to your next destination.

☐ Ride the Minnie Van service

The Walt Disney World resort has many different ways to travels from the airport and throughout the resort. The Minnie Vans offer private cars to take guests to their destination, whether it is at the beginning of their stay, visiting the theme parks and resort hotels, or Disney Springs.

These adorably decorated vehicles are a great way to see you safely through your visit to Walt Disney World.

☐ Ride the ferry boats

Guests can travel the waterways of Walt Disney World from the transportation center to the Magic Kingdom on the twin ferry boats offered. The Richard F. Irvine and Admiral Joe Fowler.

Ride along as you see Cinderella Castle in the distance growing bigger as you get closer to the entrance of the Magic Kingdom. These ferries offer guests a great view of the Polynesian resort as the Grand Floridian along the way.

☐ Travel the resort on the Walt Disney World busses

> No matter where you are at the Walt Disney World resort, you will find busses taking guests to the various hot spots. For guests staying on property, you can hop aboard any of the busses to take you to the theme parks and water parks, as well as Disney Springs.
>
> If you wish to travel to Disney Springs from the theme parks and wish to leave your vehicle in the parking area, the busses offer a great alternative.

☐ Ride the Disney Skyliner

> The Skyliner offers guests an opportunity to ride in gondolas to take you from Disney Hollywood Studios to Disney's Art of Animation resort, Disney's Caribbean Beach Resort, Disney's Pop Century Resort, or Disney's Riviera Resort.
>
> These state-of-the-art gondola's offer amazing views of the resort as you travel in comfort.

☐ Travel to and from Walt Disney World on the Disney Magical Express

> The magic of your vacation can begin long before you enter the theme parks as you hop aboard the Disney Magical Express from the airport and arrive

fresh and excited for your time at Walt Disney World.

This amazing experience includes concierge service to pick up your luggage and have it dropped in your room. Disney offers this award-winning service for a very reasonable charge.

☐ Enjoy the restaurants at any of the resort hotels

For guests looking for a dining experience outside the theme parks, the resort hotels offer a variety of dining experiences to fit any budget.

Guests looking for an authentic Polynesian feast, stop by 'Ohana, and you may even meet Stitch. 1900 Park Fare offers a beautiful character dining experience with a buffet for the whole family. Beaches and Cream Soda Shop offers an amazing old-fashioned ice cream parlor. Hoop-De-Doo Musical Revue offers a foot-stomping good time.

These are just a small sampling of the variety of dining experiences offered throughout the Walt Disney World resort. Be sure to visit the Disney World website to book your dining adventure today.

☐ Visit the water parks at Walt Disney World

Typhoon Lagoon and Blizzard Beach offer guests a great way to cool off on a hot summer day. Don your bathing suit and hop over to these themed water parks to encounter the fantastic water slides and pools offering water fun for everyone in the family.

Find the water playground for the little people in your group or try the exciting Humunga Kowabunga slide for guests who needed a bigger thrill.

☐ Visit Disney Springs

The Disney Springs District offers the best of Orlando with world-class shops, restaurants, and entertainment.

Here you will find every kind of cuisine from all American to Creole, Mexican to Italian. Whatever you crave, you will find it here.

If bowling is your thing, stop at the themed bowling alley. For fans of Lego, pop into the Lego Store to get the latest building kit to take home. Outside the Lego Store are amazing sculptures to get great pictures with.

Stop and listen to singers, musicians, and bands playing every night of the week for your enjoyment. Stop during Mardi Gras and hear traditional jazz. Visit during the holidays for ice skate and drink hot cocoa.

Whatever time of the year, there is always lots going on at Disney Springs.

- [ ] Stay at a Walt Disney World resort hotel

    Walt Disney World has resort hotels for every budget. Whether you want to stay at one of the charming All-Star resorts or looking to stay at one of the many themed hotels, check out the Walt Disney World website to see the amazing offers.

    The Polynesian gives guests a taste of the south seas while the Grand Floridian offers a grand Victorian theme. If you are interested in something with an African influence, head to the Animal Kingdom Lodge with the open beam ceilings and bamboo décor.

    Whatever your taste, you will find your favorite resort at Walt Disney World.

- [ ] Say "I Do" at Walt Disney World resort

    For the engaged couples looking for the perfect fairy tale wedding, the Walt Disney World resort offers wedding packages for every budget. From those wanting an intimate ceremony or the ultimate extravaganza, look to the wedding specialists to make your dream come true.

    Every bride will feel like a princess, and every groom will be Prince Charming at this once in a lifetime event.

One Hundred Things to do at Walt Disney World Before you Die

☐ Sail towards the sky in a hot air balloon

Disney Springs offers a unique opportunity to see the resort from a hand-painted hot air balloon. This eight-minute ride provides panoramic views of the resort for the whole family.

Do not miss this fantastic opportunity for your next vacation.

☐ Rent a Canoe, Kayak or motorboat

At the Fort Wilderness resort, guests can rent a variety of watercraft to explore the waterways of Walt Disney World. These watercraft include kayak, canoe, paddleboats, and motorboats for guests to maneuver in the enclosed waterways.

☐ Play a round of mini-golf

Join the fun with a round of mini-golf on either Winter Summerland Miniature Golf or Fantasia Gardens and Fairways Miniature Golf.

Fantasia Gardens and Fairways offer breathtaking scenes from the classic Disney film Fantasia while Winter Summerland brings a snow-covered wonderland to Florida.

Whatever your preference, you will have a great day with mini golf at Walt Disney World.

Magic Kingdom

Main Street U.S.A.

The history of Main Street U.S.A. began with Walt Disney as a young boy when his family moved from Chicago, Illinois to Marceline, Michigan, when Walt was just four years old. Walt Disney talked about his time in Marceline as his favorite time of life and revisited the family farm in 1956 with his wife, Lillian.

When Walt Disney began plans for Disneyland in 1954, he wanted his guests to experience the small town he grew up in, and thus, Main Street U.S.A. was born. While Main street has changed over the years, New shops replacing the old and new faces are smiling at guests each day. Main Street has never changed for one reason; it will always remain a thank you from Walt to his beloved Marceline.

☐ Be selected as the first family at the Magic Kingdom

> Each day before the gate of the Magic Kingdom opens, hundreds of people stand to wait for their day at this happy place to begin. While it would be enough to open the gates and let the guests explore the magic, Walt Disney World always does things in

just the right way to bring a little extra excitement to the beginning of the day.

One family is selected from the crowd and escorted to the train platform high above the multitude of people below. The cast members and characters announce this family, and they lead the crowd in the countdown to open the Magic Kingdom.

☐ Stand on the platform at the Main Street train station and get a picture of Main Street U.S.A.

The Magic Kingdom is one of the most amazing spectacles you will have the delight in seeing. While seeing the park from street level is a thrill, walking the steps to the Main Street Train Station will give you a bird's eye view of the park that will bring a chill to your skin.

Just take a few moments to revel in this beautiful view of Main Street U.S.A. with Cinderella Castle framing the picture perfectly.

☐ Visit the Main Street Station and Ride the Disney Railroad on a complete circle around the Magic Kingdom

It is a well-known fact that Walt Disney had a fascination with trains from the time he was a young child. Disney brought that love to Disneyland with the Disneyland Railroad, one of the original attractions operating since the opening day in 1955.

When the Magic Kingdom opened in 1971, the railroad would once again bring guests tremendous joy as they traveled throughout the lands of the Magic Kingdom. Whether you are moving from Main Street to other themed lands or just experiencing the Magic Kingdom from an authentic steam locomotive, traveling on the Disney railroad is a must-see for everyone.

☐ Explore Walt Disney's love of trains on the lower level of the Main Street Train Station

Walt Disney's love for trains began as a small boy in Marceline, Missouri, as he followed his uncle's passion for trains and worked on the railroad as a young boy.

As an adult, Walt continued to keep his love alive by building a scale train in the yard of his family home.

When Walt began his dream of Disneyland, the railroad was one of the first attractions engineered, and this tradition would continue here at the Magic Kingdom.

Lining the walls, you will find pictures and biographies of the Imagineers who would be immortalized in the names of the engines. Walt's wife Lillian is also immortalized in the Lillie Belle, the small caboose car that special guests and dignitaries have ridden since the beginnings of the Disney theme parks.

Authentic railroad memorabilia appear in this area, including tickets, buttons, scale models, and locks. Be sure to take some time to explore this love letter from Walt Disney to his beloved trains

- [ ] Go to City Hall and get your celebration button and birthday call from Mickey Mouse

    If you are one of the thousands of people celebrating their birthday at the Magic Kingdom, you want to make a public announcement by wearing a special birthday button. Cast members love to make these buttons customized with your age or special messages just for you. Also, Mickey Mouse is waiting to give you a special birthday message for visiting him on your special day.

    Just because it may not be your special day does not mean you cannot partake in the fun. Be sure to get your "I'm Celebrating button" to show you are with someone special. Not your birthday? Get your "Happily Ever After" button for your honeymoon or your "Graduation" button during May and June.

☐   Take one of the famous Disneyland tours

Go deeper into the history of the Magic Kingdom by taking a tour.

There have been many tours throughout the history of Walt Disney World, giving guests an inside look at the workings of the Magic Kingdom in a very personal way. The "Disney's Keys to the Kingdom" tour has been offered to guests for many years giving guests an exclusive inside look at the development of Magic Kingdom along with VIP boarding for certain attractions. While this tour changes throughout the year, the excitement of the tour remains constant. The "Disney's Family Magic" tour gives guest clues to a magical scavenger hunt throughout the theme park.

Periodically, guests will get additional thrills added to these tours like the opportunity to see Walt Disney's private apartment or ride in the Lillie Belle car on the train. These special touches add to the distinct memories each person takes with them at the end of their tour.

For guests looking for a more inclusive experience, try the "Ultimate Day of Thrills VIP" tour offering a seven-hour tour with everything you could want in a day at the Magic Kingdom.

Catherine F. Olen

☐ Ride on the Omnibus

> Weary travelers on Main Street U.S.A. can hop aboard a classic omnibus, an open-air double-decker bus that will take you right to Cinderella Castle.
>
> The omnibus offers a different view above street level, giving guests a fantastic picture opportunity of Main Street or Cinderella Castle.

☐ Travel down Main Street on the horse-drawn streetcar

> Another of the Main Street vehicles is the only non-motorized car in the livery. This antique streetcar drove guests from the entrance of Main Street to Cinderella Castle when the Magic Kingdom opened.
>
> The horse-drawn streetcar allows guests to slow down and enjoy the sights of Main Street as the streetcar is pulled by one of the Disney Clydesdales.
>
> Ask the attendant if you can pet the animals; most enjoy interacting with the guests, but remember; they are working, so please ask before approaching these magnificent horses.
>
> Keep an eye out for the Dapper Dans, as they will board the streetcar and serenade the guests traveling aboard.

- ☐ Take a ride on the Antique Firetruck

    This replica of a 1916 firetruck was added to the Main Street vehicles and takes guests from the entrance to Cinderella Castle daily. Walt Disney wanted guests to experience a real working town on Main Street U.S.A., which included working vehicles along the roadways.

    Climb aboard and ring the bell as you take a trip down Main Street U.S.A. Be sure to get an honorary fire badge sticker for your little firemen from the driver before you exit the vehicle to continue your magical day.

- ☐ Visit the Harmony Barber Shop for a haircut on your next visit

    Hidden on Main Street U.S.A. is a one of a kind experience most guests of the Magic Kingdom have no idea exists. The Harmony Barber Shop offers professional hair cutting service to guests within the Magic Kingdom. Unfortunately, this is not a shop you can walk in for a haircut. You will need to book this experience in advance.

    One of the most exciting offerings at Harmony Barber Shop is the baby's first haircut experience, including a pair of mouse ears to commemorate the occasion.

- [ ] Listen to the song stylings of The Dapper Dan's

    While the Magic Kingdom is widely known for the rides and fireworks, the entertainment cannot be compared. The Dapper Dan's have been a mainstay of Main Street U.S.A. since the park opening. Not only do the Dapper Dan's voices blend perfectly, but these talented young men also tap dance and play the organ chimes.

    You can listen to the Dapper Dan's performing daily in various places from the entrance to the Magic Kingdom. Sometimes you may even be serenaded on the streetcar or may find them singing on their bicycle built for four. No matter where you find them, it is worth time spent with The Dapper Dan's.

- [ ] Visit the Main Street Fire Station to begin your sorcerer training

    Merlin needs your help to stop Hades and the villains of the Magic Kingdom from taking over.

    Stop at the Main Street Fire Station to get your training and get your first set of cards to begin the quest to protect the kingdom. Follow the map to the various stops to cast spells to stop the villain's power from growing.

One Hundred Things to do at Walt Disney World Before you Die

☐ Visit the Town Square Theater and get your autograph from Mickey Mouse or Tinker Bell

> Inside the elaborate Town Square Theater, you will find your favorite characters waiting for you to stop by for a private meet and greet. The famous Mickey Mouse himself will be here to pose for pictures and sign your autograph book, look for his friends throughout your stay also.
>
> You may even find Peter Pan's best friend Tinker Bell here to greet guests. Do not miss this wonderful opportunity to meet your favorite Disney characters at this beautiful part of the Magic Kingdom.

☐ Have a romantic spaghetti dinner at Tony's

> Next to the Main Street Opera House, you will find a quaint Italian bistro serving the tastiest Italian food at the Magic Kingdom. Tony's hosts a fantastic array of food for any taste.
>
> As you dine, you notice the décor around you. Animation cells from the 1955 film *Lady and the Tramp*, the classic Disney film from which Tony became a part of the Disney family. The fountain of Lady and Tramp is the centerpiece of this charming restaurant.

If you look out the windows at the rear of Tony's, you will find Lady and Tramp in the alley having their intimate dinner served by Tony himself.

☐ Find the paw prints in the cement outside Tony's Italian restaurant

Lady and Tramp fell in love while Tramp helped her find her way back home in the 1955 Disney film. They have left their mark at the Magic Kingdom with a heart on the sidewalk outside Tony's Italian Restaurant with their paw prints inside.

☐ Get pictures with your favorite Disney characters on Main Street U.S.A.

Each day, thousands of guests enter the Magic Kingdom and walk through the entrance to be greeted by their favorite classic Disney characters. Mickey Mouse, Minnie Mouse, Donald Duck, Daisy Duck, Goofy, and Pluto pose for pictures and sign an autograph for the young and young at heart.

Do not miss your chance to get pictures with these icons of Disney cartoons.

☐ Be sure to pick up the most popular souvenir at the Magic Kingdom, Mouse ears.

The famous Mickey Mouse Ears have grown to offer a variety of style to suit every guest.

Throughout the history of Walt Disney World, one icon has been head and ears above the rest.

The iconic Mickey Mouse ears debuted on The Mickey Mouse Club in 1955 with children all over the United States wanting a pair of the ears as their very own. While you can no longer get your name hand-embroidered on the ears, technology has taken over to offer a variety of fonts and colors for your name.

Walt Disney World has expanded throughout the years to include hundreds of different mouse ears and headbands, including almost every character and attraction in the Disney family, as well as holiday ears and custom designs.

☐ Read the windows on the second level of the Main Street buildings

Throughout Main Street U.S.A., you will notice the second story windows have names painted on the panes of glass. While most guests will not recognize the names, Walt Disney knew each one of the names you see.

This tradition started at Disneyland resort and was brought to the Magic Kingdom to continue honoring those who worked with the Disney company. There were only three requirements when adding a new name to these Main Street buildings.

a. The person had to be retired from the company.

b. The honoree had to make a significant contribution to the company.

c. The design had to be approved by management and Imagineering.

You may even notice one window was dedicated to Elias Disney, Walt Disney's father.

☐ See the window displays of your favorite Disney films at Emporium

As you walk along the sidewalk in front of the Emporium shop on Main Street, you will notice several windows with scenes from your favorite animated Disney films adorning the windows. Find your favorite films right before your eyes with scenes from *Beauty and the Beast, The Little Mermaid, Pocahontas, Aladdin, Cinderella,* and *Snow White and the Seven Dwarfs*.

☐ Notice the illusion of the buildings on Main Street

As you walk down Main Street U.S.A., the buildings around you seem to reach up very tall. However, this is a simple use of force perspective. The first level is a full ten feet, while the second level is only eight feet tall. This creates the illusion that the buildings are much bigger than they actually are.

- [ ] Examine the street lamps as you walk down Main Street

    Most guests walking down this quaint street do not notice the street lamps lining the street but, Walt Disney World made sure no detail was too small to include at the Magic Kingdom.

    As you walk down the main street, the lamps are all gas-burning, as it was traditional during the years before electricity was readily available to most towns. As you work your way down the street towards the castle, suddenly the lamps are electric, denoting the invention of electric lights and their installation in towns across the United States.

- [ ] Visit the Main Street confectioners for sweet treats

    The Main Street Confectioners is a must-do during your time at the Magic Kingdom. Sweets of every variety are contained within the walls of this old-fashioned candy shop, but this shop has something you will not find anywhere else in the park.

    Candy artisans are busy at work daily, creating classic sweets to be sold that day. Peanut brittle, rocky road, and chocolate cover toffee are just a sample of the delights created inside for you to watch before they are packaged for you to buy.

☐ Find the old-fashioned telephone within Main Street Confectioners and listen

> Pick up the receiver on the old-fashioned phone on the wall of the Main Street Confectioners and listen to a turn of the century conversation on a party line.
>
> Back at the turn of the twentieth century, phone lines were shared, and you could pick up your phone at any time to hear another conversation or find someone eavesdropping on one of your chats. Now you can listen to the conversation in this charming candy shop.

☐ Watch the singers and dancers along Main Street greet you

> As you walk down Main Street U.S.A., you will be in for a special surprise. The residents of Main Street will travel on the horse-drawn trolley to sing and dance for you each day.
>
> Stop to listen to songs from the nineteenth century sung by talented cast members on your way down Main Street U.S.A.

☐ Listen to the Philharmonic on Main Street

> The Magic Kingdom boasts their very own Philharmonic band, and these talented musicians perform for guests each day on Main Street U.S.A. Stop and listen to your favorite Disney tunes or

traditional ragtime from the turn of the century as you work your way down Main Street.

☐ Listen to the tap-dancing lessons or singing lessons

The residents of Main Street are busy at work in their various trades. If you walk down a quiet side street by Uptown Jewelers, you can hear the vocalist trying to learn a new song or the tap-dancing class already in progress. Sit below for a few minutes to enjoy this small amusing treat.

☐ Get your picture taken with Cinderella Castle in the background

The magnificent Cinderella Castle is the crown Jewel of the Magic Kingdom. Do not miss out on getting your picture taken at various spots down Main Street as you work your way to the hub. Whether you are taking a selfie, getting a shot on your phone, or getting a PhotoPass from one of the talented photographers, you will treasure this moment when Cinderella Castle came into view.

☐ Watch the glass blowing demonstration make one-of-a-kind creations

You will not want to miss this amazing display of artistry on Main Street as you get the chance to watch the glassblower make amazing creations right in front of you.

Throughout the year, the talented glassblowers design elaborate items for guests to add to their collection or give as gifts.

☐ Visit Casey's for a hot dog after the baseball match

Inspired by the 1946 cartoon version of the poem Casey at the Bat by Ernest Lawrence Thayer, Casey's offers delicious hot dogs, drinks, and chips. Be transported back to the turn of the century with recreations of baseball memorabilia from the era as you enjoy this hearty treat.

☐ Stop and listen to the piano player at Casey's Corner

As you spend time at Casey's in the outdoor patio, you will find a white upright piano. Here you will be entertained by some of the best ragtime piano players you will have the fortune to hear.

It is not a coincidence that you recognize several classic Disney songs from your favorite films, but you will also hear classics from the turn of the century, like *The Maple Leaf Rag* by Scott Joplin.

☐ Notice the American Flags on Main Street

Most guests will notice the American Flags waving along Main Street above the buildings, but these banners are keeping a secret. None of these flags have fifty stars if you look carefully. Each flag consists of less than fifty stars, so Walt Disney World would not be required to lower every flag each evening. The only flag that is lowered is the main flag at the center of Main Street U.S.A.

☐ Watch the flag retreat ceremony every day at the Magic Kingdom

Each day at 5:00 p.m., the American Flag in Town Square is lowered and folded in a ceremony that respects not only our flag but also respects the men and women of the armed forces that visit the Magic Kingdom daily.

Join the Disneyland Band as they play patriotic tunes with the Dapper Dans and the security team offering respect to our flag in a very touching ceremony.

The men and women of the armed forces are invited to stand around the flag in places of honor.

Do not miss this ceremony each day at the Magic Kingdom.

☐ Visit First Aid for all your medical needs

While we hope no one needs the first aid facility at the Magic Kingdom during their stay, the cast members working in this area are the best in their field. Whether you need a bandage, pain killers, or more advance medical assistance, just step inside this quiet area and ask the registered nurses to help you.

These trained professionals also assist with more urgent, critical medical problems, bringing guests to help where ever you may be throughout the resort.

☐ Take a picture in front of the famous Partners statue with Walt Disney and Mickey Mouse

While Walt Disney never wanted Walt Disney World to be about himself, the cast who worked on the Magic Kingdom felt it would enhance the park to include this fantastic statue.

Dedicated on June 19, 1995, Walt Disney is holding the hand of his most famous creation, Mickey Mouse. The sculptor depicted Disney in 1960; the statue stands 6'5" while Disney only stood 5'10".

Any time of the day, you will find guests standing in line to be the next one to have their picture taken with this iconic statue with Cinderella Castle towering in the background.

☐ Enjoy breakfast with your favorite Disney characters at Crystal Palace

Each day on the patio of Plaza Inn, guests will have an amazing breakfast, but the food is not the only reason the guests make reservations for this area of the park.

During your meal, favorite Disney characters join in the fun to greet guests, sign autographs, and pose for pictures. While others can watch from the sidewalk, only those invited to the party can be included in the fun at Crystal Palace.

☐ Watch the Fireworks from Cinderella Castle

While watching the fireworks at Walt Disney World is always a magical experience, seeing them framed with Cinderella Castle is an experience you will never forget. Standing before the castle at the Magic Kingdom creates amazing memories that guests will treasure for years to come.

Watch as the dazzling explosions light up the sky over Cinderella Castle in time with your favorite Disney songs. You will not want to miss this finale for any day at the Magic Kingdom.

☐ Watch the "kiss goodnight" in front of Cinderella Castle

Each evening the Magic Kingdom wishes guests goodnight with a special kiss goodnight in front of Cinderella Castle. This short farewell combines music, lights, and narration to wish guests a safe trip home at the end of each magical day at this wonderful park.

Fantasyland

The crown jewel in the Magic Kingdom, allows guests to relive the fairy tales you grew up watching on the movie screen. With Cinderella Castle tower high above the entirety of the Magic Kingdom, just beyond her gates, you will find the stories come to life as you ride along with Peter Pan, Pinocchio, Snow White and Dumbo in this most enchanting of lands.

Stop in with Belle as she recreates your favorite story of the first time she met the Beast. Dine-in Beasts Castle and ride with the Little Mermaid as you explore her world. Take a ride in a runaway mine train or visit with your favorite characters at the circus. Anything is possible in Fantasyland.

☐ See the mosaic scene depicting the story of *Cinderella* in Cinderella castle

> Walk through the castle, and you will see the story of Cinderella told through elaborate mosaics with over three hundred thousand individual tiles used to create the scenes.

The scenes depicted through these mosaics include Cinderella with her stepmother and stepsisters at their chateau, the next shows Cinderella with her fairy godmother at the moment after she transforms the rags into a beautiful ball gown.

The third panel shows midnight at the ball, where Cinderella dashes away from the castle and her prince. The next panel displays the moment the prince places the glass slipper on Cinderella, revealing his true love, and the last panel shows the couple riding off to live happily ever after.

☐ Find the mice and birds from Cinderella watching you as you walk through the castle

Walking through Cinderella Castle is a treat, but you did not know you were being watched. The birds and mice snuck down from the attic to the tops of the columns to spy on the guests entering Fantasyland through their home.

Artists have carefully crafted these birds and mice on the tops of the columns, which demonstrates another attention to detail that creates a world of fantasy.

☐ Have dinner at Cinderella's Royal Table restaurant

High above Fantasyland is a dining experience like no other. Your experience at Cinderella's Royal Table begins as you enter the foyer. Before you climb the stairs, look up at the rafters, and you may see some of Cinderella's friends staring down at you from the heights.

Sit down to a feast in the grand dining room of the castle. Before you know it, the princesses from your favorite Disney films will personally greet you, and your little fairy godmother will get a wand and wishing star of her very own.

☐ Stay in the dream suite, the only way to sleep at the Magic Kingdom

Within Cinderella Castle is the most amazing room you could ever hope to stay in. The Dream Suite in the Magic Kingdom came into existence in 2006 during the year of a million dreams, giving special prizes to guests and allowing them to spend the night in the castle.

Since then, the suite has been opened for special tours, and no longer offered as a hotel for guests. If we wish hard enough, maybe the castle will once again open to the public.

☐ Find the statue of Cinderella near Cinderella Castle

Just outside Castle Couture, you will find a statue of princess Cinderella with her face turned down towards the ground just in front of her.

This pose of the princess was made purposefully so little princes and princesses looking at the statue will see Cinderella looking directly at them instead of looking above their heads. Another reason is included in the mosaic just behind this statue. If you look carefully, there is a crown in the background that aligns perfectly with Cinderella's head if you are at child height. Next time you are at this statue, kneel and get an amazing photograph.

☐ Meet the characters from Cinderella at Cinderella Castle

Meeting the princesses is always a treat at the Magic Kingdom, but did you know you can meet the characters from Cinderella inside Fantasyland at the castle?

Lady Tremaine and Cinderella's stepsisters Anastasia and Drizella are trying to find fans to like them the best as they pose for pictures.

When Cinderella's stepfamily is not there, you can meet the fairy godmother and get a hug before a memorable picture to take home as a souvenir.

☐ Make a wish at Cinderella's wishing well

Hidden within Fantasyland is the royal wishing well just to the side of Cinderella Castle. Close your eyes and drop your penny in the well while you wish for your heart's desire. As you stand before the well, notice the mice around the base being chased by Lady Tremaine's cat, Lucifer.

- [ ] Visit Merida at Fairytale Gardens

    Merida has come to Fantasyland to sign autographs for guests of the Magic Kingdom. This princess from Scotland brings traditional décor and tartan for guests to see as she chats and takes pictures. Do not miss this great meet and greet on your next visit.

- [ ] Stop at Castle Couture and see princess Aurora's enchanted gown

    One of the first shops you will come to in Fantasyland is the Castle Couture shop. Within this shop, magic awaits as you find the gown Princess Aurora wore in *Sleeping Beauty*. Watch as this enchanted gown changes from pink to blue and back again, waiting for Aurora to wear it again. Listen carefully, and you will hear the good fairies arguing over which color looks best on the dress.

    If you continue looking through the rooms of this shop, you will also find the pink gown that once belonged to Cinderella's mother. This gown is awaiting the birds and mice to finish it before Cinderella returns from her chores.

One last detail within Castle Couture is hanging on the walls. You will notice silhouette's framed throughout this store of each of your favorite princesses.

☐ Visit Sir Mickey's and see if you can catch a glimpse of Willie the Giant

Inside Fantasyland, a charming shop stands as a love letter to Mickey Mouse cartoons, *The Brave Little Tailor* and *Mickey and the Beanstalk*.

Throughout this shop, you will notice little hints about Mickey's occupation. Notice the spools of thread and the clock with a scissors used for the hands.

You might feel like you are being watched while inside Sir Mickey's. Take a look at where the roof meets the wall, and you will find none other than Willie the Giant looking inside from the roof.

If you ask nicely, maybe he will change into a little pink bunny or even a fly for you.

☐ Visit with your favorite princesses at the Princess Fairytale Hall

Princes and Princesses travel far and wide to meet with the princesses at the Princess Fairytale Hall in Fantasyland.

Meet with Cinderella, Sleeping Beauty, Rapunzel, Tiana, and Elena in a royal setting. Be sure to bring your autograph book and your camera to immortalize this magical moment.

☐ Be a part of the audience at Mickey's PhilharMagic and see your favorite songs come to life

Join Mickey Mouse for a concert unlike any other when you hear your favorite Disney songs come to life. Watch out for Donald Duck as he spends his time playing with Mickey's sorcerer's hat instead of setting up for the concert.

Join Aladdin and Jasmine, Simba, Ariel, Lumiere, and Peter Pan, recreating songs from their films while Donald does his best to get in the way.

Spend some time in the lobby reading the posters for the new shows, including Torch Songs with Hades; Genie sings the blues, Wheezy in his final squeaks, and Willie the Whale in I, Pagliacci.

☐ Ride on Prince Charming's Regal Carousel

The centerpiece of Fantasyland is Prince Charming's Regal Carousel. Built in 1917, this antique was initially called The Liberty Carousel when it was in operation at Bell Isle Park in Detroit, Michigan.

Originally this carousel was called Cinderella's Royal Carousel but was renamed in 2010. When asked why the carousel has been renamed, the Disney Company gave the backstory of Prince Charming, after he and Cinderella married, he practiced jousting on a small circular contraption with wooden horses. The villagers became enamored with the small device and wanted to try for themselves. The prince built a larger version and gave it to the people of the kingdom.

☐ Meet with the Seven Dwarfs and ride on a runaway mine train

Spend some time with Snow White and her seven dwarfs as you explore the mine and see them hard at work along with their woodland friends.

Hold on tight as your mine train takes off on a speedy romp through the mountain hiding the mine within.

Finally, peek in the window of the dwarf's cottage and watch Snow White dancing with the dwarfs in a happy moment from one of your favorite stories.

☐ Visit the hundred-acre wood with The Many Adventures of Winnie the Pooh

Travel through the pages of your favorite stories to see Winnie the Pooh, Tigger, Piglet, Eeyore, and

Rabbit in the adventures you have known since childhood.

Get swept away in a flood from the rainstorm, get blown away on a blustery day, and fight Heffalumps and Woozles to keep Pooh's honey safe.

☐ See Mr. Toad hand the deed to his property to Owl in The Many Adventures of Winnie the Pooh

Before the friends of the hundred-acre wood came to the Magic Kingdom, Mr. Toad and his friends amused guests of all ages at Mr. Toad's Wild Ride.

Hidden within the Many Adventures of Winnie the Pooh, you will find a framed picture of Owl and Mr. Toad in which Mr. Toad is handing over the deed to the property you are riding through.

This is another example of the attention to detail the Imagineers at the Disney parks have given throughout each attraction.

☐ Ride with the Mad Hatter and Dormouse on The Mad Tea Party

Step into the pages of *Alice in Wonderland* and take a ride on The Mad Tea Party.

The Mad Hatter has invited you to his tea as you ride around the teapot that holds the Dormouse.

For those looking for a thrill, see how fast you can get your teacup spinning before your ride is through.

☐ Step through the home of the Darlings and into the nursery of Wendy, John, and Michael

Before you take off for Neverland with Peter Pan and Tinker Bell, take some time to explore the yard and nursery of the Darling children. Say hello to Nana, the Darlings dog, and nursemaid to the children before you enter the house.

Within the nursery, among the toys, look closely, and you will find Tinker Bell playing in the toy boat or spinning the globe. Tink needs to watch out as she bumps into a painting but spends a little time straightening it before continuing her exploration. Find the blocks that spell out Peter Pan on Michael's bed showing their fascination with the hero from their bedtime stories.

Interact with the shadows on the wall. Ring the bells or play with the butterflies that appear and disappear in the light.

☐ Fly with Peter Pan, Tinker Bell, Wendy, John and Michael to Neverland

Board a pirate ship and fly with Wendy, Peter, and Michael Darling over the rooftops of London to Neverland. There you will go to war with Indians, swim with mermaids, and fight Captain Hook and his band of pirates before flying home.

☐ Join the children around the world on It's a Small World

Join the happiest cruise in all of the Magic Kingdom as you travel the nations of the world singing this anthem to goodwill, *It's a Small World After All.*

This attraction initially premiered on May 30, 1966, at Disneyland with Walt Disney creating a gala event with children pouring water from all of the oceans of the world into the canal of this attraction to bring all the waters of the world together in the way Walt Disney wanted to bring people together.

☐ Meet with Belle at her chateau and be transformed to Beast castle through the enchanted mirror in Enchanted Tales with Belle

Visit the small home of Belle and her father in a peaceful village where they live. In the main room, find dozens of Belle's books stacked about and the growth chart on the wall showing Belle's height as she grows.

Spend some time in the workshop of her father, Maurice, before magic brings you to Beast's castle to see Belle and relive the tale of *Beauty and the Beast*.

One Hundred Things to do at Walt Disney World Before you Die

☐   Eat at the Beast's castle at Be Our Guest

High on a hill overlooking Fantasyland stands the castle of the beast. Walk over the drawbridge and through the doors to enter a world where the servants are everyday items, and the enchanted rose is under the bell jar when you eat at Be Our Guest.

Listen to the suits of armor chat as you wait for your order to be taken. Sit in the grand ballroom and watch as the snow falls outside on the mountains.

Spend some time in the music box room and examine the tapestries and paintings of Belle's life at the castle.

For those brave enough to enter the west wing, eat in the Beasts dark part of the castle where the enchanted rose and the magic portrait are hidden.

☐   Stop in at Gaston's for an apple freeze

In the small French village that is the backdrop for the fairytale of Beauty and the Beast, you will find the rustic tavern of Gaston.

Inside, find the large fireplace and sit in the enormous chair waiting for Gaston's return from the hunt.

Sit among the antler décor and have a refreshing apple freeze. For a unique souvenir, get this tasty drink in a stein to take home with you.

☐ Be one of the lucky ones to meet Gaston

Throughout the square in the small village, you will find evidence of how much Gaston loves his contribution to the people he lives near.

From time to time, Gaston will take time out from hunting to commune with the guests and give them a thrill by posing for pictures and signing autographs. Don't miss this opportunity to meet with this legendary figure, just ask him.

☐ Ride in a clamshell to join in Ariel's adventures in The Journey of the Little Mermaid

Another castle in Fantasyland is the home of Prince Eric and Ariel from *The Little Mermaid*. Down below the castle, you will find a clamshell that will take you down into the depths of the ocean as you relive the story with Ariel and her friends Scuttle, Sebastien and Flounder.

Watch out for Ursula and her eels along your journey and celebrate with the rest of King Triton's subjects at the marriage of Ariel ad Eric.

☐ Meet with the Little Mermaid at Ariel's Grotto

Now you can meet with Ariel face to face at Ariel's Grotto. Spend some time with this red-headed princess as she signs autographs and poses for photos with guests all through the day.

☐ Take pictures with King Triton statue

Just across from the Adventures of the Little Mermaid, guests will find Seafarers Wood Carvers with the giant half-completed statue of King Triton standing outside.

Guests can pose for pictures with this stunning statue before entering Seafarer's to see the artist's renderings of this statue in the planning stage. Be sure to spend a few minutes with this beautiful piece of art.

☐ Meet your favorite Disney pals at Pete's Silly Sideshow

Join the circus sideshow with Pete's as you find your favorite Disney characters getting ready for their circus acts in Storybook Circus.

Goofy poses for pictures as you see his motorcycle daredevil act has gone a little wrong. Donald Duck is the snake charmer, posing with Kaa from *The Jungle Book*. Daisy tells your fortune as the gypsy, and Minnie poses with her French poodles as the dog trainer.

Be sure to bring your autograph book, so you include their signatures before you go.

☐ Find the circus animal tracks in the ground along with the Storybook Circus

All along the path at the Storybook Circus, you will find the paw prints of the circus animals walking through to the big top.

☐ Spend time in the big top before riding with Dumbo the Flying Elephant

The big top is waiting for your little one to come and play as you wait for your time to fly with Dumbo.

Inside, you will find Dumbo flying high above the center ring as the circus goes on below him. Slide down the human cannonball as you steer clear of the tower of flames before leaving the big top to spend time flying above the circus with Dumbo.

☐ Take off with daredevil Goofy and learn to fly at the Barnstormer

Thrill seeker, the Great Goofini, wants to take you along on his latest dangerous stunt as he flies in his Barnstormer plane.

Along the queue, do not miss Goofini's enormous human cannonball and see where he literally hit his target.

Next, board a plane for a high-speed flight around the circus. He hopes you make it back in one piece.

- [ ] Cool off on a hot day at the circus train

    Right in the center of the Storybook Circus, you will find the happiest animals ever to ride the train to Fantasyland.

    Get soaking wet with the Giraffes, Elephants, and Monkeys as they squirt you in every way imaginable to cool you off on a warm day. Be careful of these critters if the weather turns colder as they will not give up their mission to get you wet every day.

- [ ] Visit the Rapunzel themed area of Fantasyland

    Guests walking from Fantasyland to Liberty Square will find a charming little area that has come straight out of the Disney film *Tangled*. Rapunzel has been working hard at painting the buildings, and her friends are helping by leaving their mark on this quaint area of Fantasyland.

- [ ] Take pictures with the floating lanterns

    An extraordinary photo opportunity can only be found in the Tangled area of Fantasyland. After dark, guests can post with a floating lantern to get a very special souvenir of their day in the Magic Kingdom.

☐ Find the present from Flynn Rider left for Maximus

> In the Tangled area of Fantasyland, guests will find a bag of apples resting atop one of the barrels. This particular detail is straight out of the film when Flynn Rider leaves a large bag of apples for Maximus, the horse at the end of the film.

☐ Find Maximus hoof prints in the Tangled area of Fantasyland

> Throughout the Magic Kingdom, guests will notice areas where the characters leave behind a footprint, paw prints, or wheel marks. Within the Tangled area, the hoof prints have the name Maximus printed at the top. Maximus, the horse, has been in this area, perhaps looking for Flynn Rider or his bag of apples.

☐ Read the wanted posters in the Tangled area

> On the buildings of the Tangled area of Fantasyland, you will find wanted posters for the ruffians that Rapunzel met at the Snuggly Duckling. Upon closer inspection, you will see these are not for wanted men, but advertisements for their various talents.

Liberty Square

Travel back to the early days of the United States of America as you rediscover the roots of American history. Walt Disney's passion for his country began when he joined the Army and drove an ambulance during World War I.

Included in every theme park, Disney has celebrated the history that made this country great. Listen to the great words of the president that influenced Disney throughout his life, Abraham Lincoln. Ride along the Rivers of America to learn about the native people and our great land.

Listen to the stories of our country and taste how the colonials lived during your visit to Liberty Square.

☐ Read the bronze plaque on the bridge from Main Street

> As guests cross over from Main Street to Liberty Square, they may notice a small bronze plaque on the right brick pillar of the small bridge. Stop for a moment to read the words as they tell the story

of the colonist who gave the ultimate sacrifice to protect their new country from the interests of England.

Take a moment to read about these people and enter the area dedicated to the origins of the United States of America.

☐ Grab a sweet treat at Sleepy Hollow

One of the best-kept secrets at the Magic Kingdom stands just across the bridge into Liberty Square. Stop at Sleepy Hollow for Mickey waffles or funnel cake with strawberries and whipped cream for a wonderful sweet treat during your time in Liberty Square. For those looking for a hearty meal, try a corn dog or an egg and cheese waffle sandwich for a great breakfast.

Be sure to notice the emblem on the sign above. You will see the classic Headless Horseman character from the Washing Irving poem, which Disney immortalized in 1949, starring the voice of crooner Bing Crosby.

☐ Join our Presidents in the Hall of Presidents to hear the immortal words of history

Originally, Walt Disney wanted an attraction similar to Great Moments with Mr. Lincoln at Disneyland in California. Unfortunately for Disney, the technology of the time was not sophisticated enough to grant him his dream of the attraction.

However, when Walt Disney World opened in 1971, the Imagineers were able to realize Disney's dream fully.

Any history of this attraction would need to start with the building in which it is housed. The Hall of Presidents building is built to resemble Independence Hall in Philadelphia in Pennsylvania. When you enter the building, stop in the center of the room to admire the Presidential Seal in the rug. The Magic Kingdom is the only place in the world outside of the White House and government buildings where the Presidential Seal is displayed.

☐ Visit the Liberty Tree with the thirteen lanterns signifying the thirteen original colonies of the United States

Towering above Liberty Square stands the Liberty Tree, a replica of the tree in Boston, where the colonists assembled to discuss the events before the Boston Tea Party.

The 1957 Disney film *Johnny Tremaine* chronicles the life of young Tremaine in the days leading up to the revolutionary war. In one scene, the colonists hang lanterns in the tree to signify the thirteen colonies. This replica gives guests an up-close experience of those colonists so many years ago.

☐ Find the two lanterns in the window signifying two if by sea

Along the quiet lane of Liberty Square, notice the windows of the charming homes. If you look carefully, you will find one window with two lanterns standing quietly within. This symbol pays homage to the poem, *The Midnight Ride of Paul Revere,* and waits for guests to take notice during their time in this small village.

☐ Find the small doll in the window of one of the colonist homes

This was a signal to the army that a child lives in this home. During the tumultuous times of the colonists, it was important for firefighters and villagers to know that children lived in this home.

The Imagineers paint a very detailed picture for guests throughout the Magic Kingdom, and this is just another example of the loving care brought forth by the Walt Disney Company.

☐ Find the replica of the Liberty Bell

In the Liberty Square area, you will find a copy of the Liberty Bell cast to exact specifications. The original Liberty Bell is housed across the from Independence Hall in Philadelphia, but you can experience this piece of history during your time at the Magic Kingdom.

Legend says that this bell was donated by the state of Pennsylvania as they have the original housed in Philadelphia, so their copy was brought to Walt Disney World to be displayed here.

☐ Visit the original flags of the thirteen colonies

Surrounding the area where the Liberty Bell is housed, you will find thirteen flags signifying the original thirteen colonies. Each flag is a replica of the original flag from the British colonies that began in the seventeenth and eighteenth centuries. Included are Delaware, Pennsylvania, New Jersey, Connecticut, Georgia, Massachusetts, Maryland, South Carolina, New Hampshire, Virginia, New York, North Carolina, and Rhode Island.

☐ Eat at Liberty Tree Tavern

Go back in time to this quaint tavern where you can find delicious fare from the colonial times. Whether you crave pot roast, roast turkey, or battered fish and chips, you will find a delicious meal in a charming setting.

Be sure to try Johnny Appleseed's warm apple cake or Ooey Gooey Toffee Cake for dessert.

☐ Take a ride on the Liberty Square Riverboat around the Rivers of America

Ride aboard the Liberty Belle Riverboat along the Rivers of America while experiencing the history of this majestic river. Enjoy the sights of the riverfront while your narrator gives you the story of Liberty Square, Frontierland, and Tom Sawyer Island. Keep a weathered eye out for native American Indians living along the river banks on your travels.

☐ Stand in the stocks for a great picture

Within Liberty Square, find the strange wooden device with three holes, one for your head and two for your arms. This device was used during colonial times to punish townsfolks for a variety of offenses.

People would be subjected publicly to the torment of the townsfolk for their crimes, including tickling, while the punished person was helpless to stop the torture.

☐ Get your picture taken with the haunted mansion or antique funeral coach at the Haunted Mansion

Before embarking on your tour of this haunted home, stop for a photo with the façade of this estate in the background. You may even find additional guests in your picture with PhotoPass.

Get a picture with the antique funeral coach before it is needed again for yet another funeral procession.

☐ Visit the cemetery in the queue for the Haunted Mansion

As you explore the property on which the Haunted Mansion sits, you will be given plenty of time to explore the cemetery where generations of the family of Master Gracey are laid to rest.

Centered in this graveyard is the grave of the great master himself. Be sure to spend a moment to revere the building of the mansion before you.

Be careful as you tour the cemetery, you may get wet by the ghost of the sea captain or accidentally play a tune on the granite musical instruments. Stop and recite some poetry before you are done and watch out because the eyes of the dead may be watching you before you enter this quiet estate.

☐ Visit the 999 happy haunts at the Haunted Mansion.

Are you brave enough to explore the rooms of this long-abandoned estate where the only residents are those that have left this earthly realm for a long time? Nine-hundred and ninety-nine happy haunts greet you throughout the house as you explore the library, music room, stair to nowhere, the halls, and finally, the séance room where Madam Leota brings the spirits to relive their time in the mansion.

Explore the dining room where a feast is held, and dancers' whirl in an endless ball before coming face to face with Master Gracey's bride in the attic. Explore the cemetery while ghosts sing for your pleasure.

Be careful, or you may pick up unwanted hitchhikers before you finish your tour.

☐ Read the epitaphs on the crypts outside the Haunted Mansion

Before your time at the Haunted Mansion is done, stop to read the epitaphs of the dead outside the exit to this estate. You may chuckle out loud as you read some of the names engraved on the crypt fronts.

☐ Find the grave of a beloved Disney character in the pet cemetery on the hillside

Human guests are not the only ones laid to rest at this sprawling manor. The pet cemetery stands in memorial to all of the lost pets throughout the generations. If you look high on this hillside, you may find the grave of an iconic Disney character, Mr. Toad, in his classic pose.

- [ ] Find the elusive Madame Leota at the Memento Mori Shop near the Haunted Mansion

    As you enter the Memento Mori shop, you will find several nods to the infamous Madame Leota. Stand before the mirror within this shop, and you may be face to face with this woman and truly in touch with the spirit realm.

- [ ] Find the glowing spirits within Memento Mori

    As you peruse the shelve of this shop, look at some of the jars above your head. From time to time, you may find colorful, glowing spirits taking residence within these vessels before dimming and disappearing once again.

- [ ] Notice the brown strip running down the center of the street in Liberty Square

    Many guests who visit Liberty Square never notice the strip of brown running through the center of the street in this quaint area. But this discolored section has a real-world purpose.

    Back in colonial times, the colonists threw their waste outside the window to run down the street. Since these colonists did not live with indoor plumbing, there were no other choices, and this was the norm in this era.

True to history, the Magic Kingdom has included this little detail to allow guests to experience the colonies in the exact way the people living in the age would have lived.

☐ Try to find a restroom within the Liberty Square area

Guests will find restrooms throughout the Magic Kingdom, but guests may have a difficult time finding one within this area of the theme park.

Liberty Square is the only area without restrooms since there were no restrooms in colonial America. In keeping with the historical aspects of this land, Disney opted not to include modern conveniences.

☐ Visit Ye Olde Christmas Shoppe in Liberty Square

Souvenir are everywhere in the Magic Kingdom, but for those looking for Christmas at any time of the year, Ye Olde Christmas Shoppe offers a wide variety of Christmas décor.

Get your ornament personalized by the talented artists in this shop.

Frontierland

Step back to the origins of the United States as you enter Frontierland. Walkthrough the streets of a frontier town and learn about the origins of the settlers. Join the show at the Diamond Horseshoe or try your hand at some fancy shooting at the Frontierland Shootin' Gallery.

Travel on an authentic paddleboat around the Rivers of America or ride through the wilderness on a run-away train. Top off your time in Frontierland with a ride on Splash Mountain with your friends from *Song of the South*.

☐ Visit the Frontierland Shootin' Arcade and try your hand at some fancy shooting

Fill your gun and aim at the graves on Boot Hill Cemetery. Light up the sky and bring the animals of the frontier to life as you try some fancy shooting at this old-fashioned shooting gallery.

As you hit the targets, read some of the humorous epitaphs that appear along with clever animation throughout this precursor to the modern video games.

☐ Cross the Rivers of America on an old fashion raft over to Tom Sawyer Island

At the shore of the Rivers of America, you will find a small dock with a raft waiting to take guests across the river to play on Tom Sawyer Island. This attraction has been a working part of Disney parks since the earliest years of Disneyland.

This short trip is reminiscent of the raft Huckleberry Finn took in the famous book by Mark Twain. Spend some time whitewashing the fence, playing among the caverns, and exploring the secret tunnels in the fort after your crossing to the island.

☐ Explore the island where Tom Sawyer and Huckleberry Finn ran with Becky

Go back to a simpler time where kids used their imagination to create new worlds all around them. Step through the pages of *The Adventures of Huckleberry Finn* to explore the island. Pretend you are Tom Sawyer or Becky Thatcher as you become the hero of this Mark Twain classic.

☐ Locate the whitewashed fence that Tom hasn't finished

Along Tom Sawyer Island, you will find a large stretch of fence that appears to be partially painted white with the words Tom and Becky painted on it. For those that have never read the Mark Twain classic, *The Adventures of Huckleberry Finn*, this may seem strange, but Walt Disney wanted to include many types of history within his theme park, including fictional history.

In the story, Tom is told by his aunt to paint her 30 x 9-foot fence. This would be eight-hundred square feet of fencing, too much for a young boy.

Tom tricks his friends into believing this is fun and pay him for the privilege of doing the chore for him. Here before you, stands that very fence waiting to be finished.

☐ Find the bear claw marks in the lobby of the Country Bear Jamboree

While waiting to enter the theater for the Country Bear Jamboree look around at the portraits of some of the entertainers framed on the walls of the lobby.

Most guests miss a detail left behind by the very bears that will be singing for you in a few moments. Look at the floor, and you will see claw marks left on the wood floors by the country bears.

☐ Enjoy some good old foot-stompin' fun at the Country Bear Jamboree

Join the country bears in Grizzly Hall to listen to your favorite songs from the origins of the United

States. This show is one of the original attractions on the opening day of the Magic Kingdom, and the Country Bear Jamboree has been entertaining guests for almost fifty years.

Hear your host, Henry, as he introduces you to the performers and interacts with his permanent audience Buff, Max, and Melvin the trophy heads in the theater. Meet Gomer, the piano player, Wendell, and Liver Lips.

The female performers in the cast include Bunny, Bubbles, and Beulah, the Sun Bonnet Trio, Trixie and, the star of the show, Teddy Berra.

Stomp your feet and clap along with the music as you enjoy this Frontierland classic attraction.

☐ Take a ride on Splash Mountain and fall fifty feet into the briar patch

Another mountain peak to grace the mountain range of Walt Disney World is Splash Mountain. Walk through the old barn to board a hollow log and explore the wilderness that makes up this delighted mountain.

Along your way, you will find some friends from the Disney classic *Song of the South*. Br'er Fox and Br'er Bear are trying to catch Br'er Rabbit for their supper. Hopefully, you can help this little rabbit from getting caught.

Find Mr. Blue Bird and sing along to a classic Disney tune before climbing the peak to Br'er Foxes lair. Hold on when you fall fifty feet into the briar patch below to escape with your life.

Finish your time at Splash Mountain by celebrating with all of Br'er Rabbits friends as they celebrate.

☐ Listen for the gophers to salute Florida State University

As your ride on Splash Mountain reaches the climax before the hill to the final drop, you will hear several gophers pop their heads out to giggle. If you listen carefully, you will hear the last gopher yell FSU. This little detail is Disney's way of celebrating Florida State University.

☐ Sit in the rocking chairs inside the Briar Patch

Just to the left of the Splash Mountain entrance, you will find a small shop, the Briar Patch. When you enter this shop, a large fireplace stands in the center of the room with two wooden rocking chairs waiting for weary guests to take a seat and rest.

Most days, you will find guests who have already claimed this spot for themselves but keep an eye out, and you may have a turn in these comfortable chairs.

☐ Find the painting of Whistler's Mother with a small addition in the Briar Patch

Spend some time looking at the rooms of the bunny house and find the picture of Whistler's Mother compete with bunny ears.

The famous painting of Whistler's Mother, painted in 1871 by renowned artist James McNeill has become an icon of American Art, and now it appears the bunny family has included this painting in their home décor.

☐ Visit the Briar Patch store and find the barrel of laughs

One of the hidden gems in this quaint shop is the barrel behind the counter with a smile painted on it. It is quite literally a barrel of laughs.

☐ Check out the mining operator in the queue for Big Thunder Mountain Railroad

The Big Thunder Mountain Railroad queue is packed full of fun even before you begin your ride. While in line, you will find a portrait of the founder, Barnabas T. Bullion. The picture, however, is that of imaginer Tony Baxter. Later you will find the crates of explosives waiting for the workers. Western River Expedition was a never realized attraction given a little nod within the queue of this beloved attraction.

Further, within the queue, you will find the pay rates signed by none other than G. Willikers. Stop for a moment to look at the shaft diagram. The shaft is #71, the year the Magic Kingdom opened.

Find the advertisement for the Hard Times Café, the name of the café from the Walt Disney Classic, *The Apple Dumpling Gang*.

Be sure to interact with the canaries to ensure the workers can breathe safely. You may even find one with the name Rosita, the missing bird from the Enchanted Tiki Room.

☐ Read the names on the trains on the Big Thunder Mountain Railroad out loud

The six trains on this attraction have some very unusual names. As you being boarding, stop and read some of the names like I.M. Fearless, U.R. Courageous, U.B. Bold, I.B. Hearty, U.R. Daring, and I.M. Brave.

- [ ] Ride through the wild west on the Big Thunder Mountain Railroad

    Climb aboard an old fashioned mine train and take a wild ride through Big Thunder Mountain. During your journey, guests will find underground caves, mining tunnels, hot springs, as well as mining equipment throughout. Your ride will send you screaming around the tracks and up the mining shafts before delivering you safely back to the mining office.

- [ ] Find the secret Tinker Bell at Big Thunder Mountain Railroad

    Cast members have confirmed that there is a profile of Tinker Bell carved into the rock by the left side of the exit. While this may be difficult to see, take a few minutes to find Tinker Bell's wing, and you may be able to make out the rest of this tiny fairy.

- [ ] Examine the buildings throughout Frontierland to see architecture throughout the history of the old west

    As you wander through the streets of Frontierland, you may notice each building has a date included on the façade.

    These dates are not just random; each date coincides with a particular type of architecture from that period.

☐ Stop at Pecos Bill and find items left behind by your favorite characters

> The Pecos Bill Tall Tale Inn and Café have some of the tastiest food at the Magic Kingdom, but the story behind this restaurant is much more than guests realize.
>
> Within the restaurant, you will find several leather parchments with the story of Pecos Bill, the toughest cowboy in the west.
>
> Continue your exploration of this building, and you will find most of Bill's friends have stopped by and left some of their signature items behind.
>
> Johnny Appleseed's pot hat, Paul Bunyon's ax, Davy Crockett's powder horn, and the Lone Ranger's mask are just a few of the items you will find while enjoying Pecos Bill Tall Tale Inn and Café.

☐ Watch the parades from the streets of Frontierland

> The parades are an iconic part of the Walt Disney World experience, but it can be challenging to find a perfect viewing spot along the Main Street area.
>
> Guests may have a better view of the parade by making their way to the streets of Frontierland to see the parade pass by.

Adventureland

Get ready to explore the wilds of the jungle when you travel to exotic places to test your limits.

See how the Swiss family Robinson survived their shipwreck and live on this island hideaway as you climb to the treetops above Adventureland. Travel down the rivers of the world with your Jungle Cruise river guide or dare to enter the caverns below Adventureland with the Pirates of the Caribbean.

Whatever speaks to the adventurer in you, you will have a wild time in Adventureland.

☐ Visit the Robinson family dwelling at the Swiss Family Robinson Treehouse

Join the Robinson family in their treetop abode as you rediscover a Walt Disney classic. This attraction, inspired by the 1960 film *Swiss Family Robinson*, the story of a family shipwrecked and surviving on a deserted island.

This enormous tree holds their bed chambers, dining room, living area, and a kitchen complete with furniture salvaged from the shipwreck.

☐ Enjoy a refreshing Dole Whip

One of the favorite snacks at the Magic Kingdom can be found within the Adventureland area. Dole Whip offers a cold pineapple flavored refreshment in a cup or a Dole Whip float.

Be sure to stop at Aloha Isle to get your pineapple Dole Whip on your next visit to the Magic Kingdom.

☐ Try an orange citrus swirl at Sunshine Tree Terrace

For guests who prefer the refreshing taste of orange, you can try the orange citrus swirl at Sunshine Tree Terrace near the Swiss Family Robinson treehouse.

☐ Be careful of the camels surrounding the Magic Carpet Ride; they just might spit at you

Centered in Adventureland, you will find the Magic Carpets of Aladdin attraction complete with golden camels surrounding. If you are not looking closely as you pass by, these camels may just get you wet as they spit at you.

☐ Ride on a magic carpet above the streets of Agrabah on the Magic Carpets of Aladdin

Take off on a magic carpet ride straight out of your favorite film, *Aladdin*. Fly over the streets of Adventureland, just like Aladdin and Jasmine flew around the world, seeing the wonders for themselves.

☐ Explore the open-air market in Adventureland

Throughout the area around the Magic Carpets of Aladdin, guests will find a Bazaar with wonders for you to take home. Be sure to look at the clothing with dazzling patterns, sunglasses, or toys from your favorite Disney films packed into this area.

☐ Meet with your favorite Adventureland characters

Guests never know who they may run into as they explore Adventureland. Be sure to keep an eye out for the Genie, Aladdin, and Jasmine as they sign autographs and pose for pictures with guests on their land. The gang from the *Lion King* is waiting for you as well as Peter Pan, and Captain Hook, so have your autograph books ready for a chance encounter with your favorite characters.

☐ Meet with the singing birds and flowers in The Enchanted Tiki Room

The birds and flowers of the Tiki room were some of the first animatronics developed for Disneyland along with Great Moments with Mr. Lincoln, and It's a Small World.

The anthem for the Tiki Room was written by the Sherman Brothers, who are known for writing songs for *Mary Poppins* starring Julie Andrews and *Bed Knobs and Broomsticks* starring Angela Lansbury.

This marked the first time in Disneyland history that a song was written specifically for an attraction. The Tiki Room has remained the same since the premiere in June 1963.

☐ Check out the captive tarantula spider in the queue for The Jungle Cruise

Throughout the queue for the Jungle Cruise, you will find a fun tongue in cheek jokes to entertain the guests. As you get closer to the loading dock, you will find a small cage with a tarantula inside. Spend some time examining this tiny creature, but be careful or you just might lose a finger.

☐ Travel the rivers of the jungle with your expert guide on The Jungle Cruise

Explore the rivers of the jungle with your expert skipper and marvel at the wonders you will see on the rivers of the world. Travel down the river to the African savannah, where you will see animals at the river's edge. Find the lost safari group or watch as the gorillas take over the camp.

Wonder at a native tribe, but be careful so you do not get ambushed. Finally, see the eighth wonder of the world before you head back to civilization.

☐ Stop for a moment to see the orangutan that has escaped from his crate as you exit the Jungle Cruise

Before exiting the Jungle Cruise, stop and look at some of the crates waiting for the next expedition through the jungle.

Find the crate labeled This End Up; there seems to be some confusion as to which end this should be.

Very low to the ground stands a crate that contains a giant poisonous spider, but the seal seems to be broken.

The centerpiece of these mismanaged crates seems to be the orangutan cage, but the occupant is missing.

It is a good thing you came back in on piece.

☐ Cool off as the Tikis spray you with water

As you wander the streets of Adventureland, you will find a set of tiki statues and a crowd of people standing nearby in the warmer months. These tikis statues offer a cooling mist that is very refreshing on a hot day.

☐ Hang out around the Pirates of the Caribbean, and you just might see the one and only Captain Jack Sparrow

Near the Pirates of the Caribbean attraction, you may have an encounter with real live pirates. The famous Captain Jack Sparrow and his band of marauders regularly visit to recruit new pirates from the guests in the crowd.

Be sure to bring your autograph book and camera to take pictures with the greatest pirate of them all.

☐ Find the pirates playing chess in the queue for Pirates of the Caribbean

When you approach the queue for this attraction, you will notice it splits off into two directions.

The fast pass queue travels around a jail cell one floor below you. These two pirate skeletons seem to be deadlocked in a game of chess.

Rumor has it that the chess pieces are arranged on the board in a stalemate because the pirates died while playing this game.

☐ Ride along with Pirates of the Caribbean as you travel the waters and see the cursed treasure

Travel through dark, haunted caverns before plunging to where the remains of pirates stand silently below the ground.

Be careful if you spy the cursed treasure, or you may be sent back to the time of Pirates. Help Captain Barbossa locate Captain Jack Sparrow while pirates loot the city. Can you escape before the city is destroyed?

☐ Explore the Bazaar in the exit of Pirates of the Caribbean

Explore this open-air bazaar at the exit of Pirates of the Caribbean and find your perfect pirate-themed items. Find the pirate within you with a T-shirt, eye patch, saber, or toy to remind you of your time on Pirates of the Caribbean.

☐ Play A Pirates Adventure – Treasures of the Seven Seas

Guests can help Captain Jack Sparrow find the elusive treasure with clues left around the area of

Pirates of the Caribbean. Pick up the magic Talisman to bring your adventure on your next travels through Adventureland.

☐ Grab a bite to eat or a refreshing drink at Tortuga Tavern

Across the walkway from the Pirates of the Caribbean, you can find a quiet tavern with food and drinks ready for marauding pirates.

Pirate booty lines the walls, and Blackbeard, the Pirates look at guests from the mural near the topping bar.

Sit in the Captain Jack Sparrow dining room, and you will find the crew roster for the Black Pearl and Queen Anne's Revenge. Blackbeard's crew have signed their lives away to the seas. Notice the Black Pearl captain has conspicuously crossed out Barbossa and added the name of Captain Jack Sparrow in its place.

Tomorrowland

Get ready to rocket into the future as you explore the furthest reaches of space at Tomorrowland.

When the Magic Kingdom opened in 1971, Tomorrowland opened with only two attractions, the Grand Prix Raceway and the Skyway to Fantasyland.

Today, Tomorrowland offers guests a full exploration of the future with a trip on Space Mountain. Ride along with Buzz Lightyear to save the galaxy from evil Emperor Zurg. Ride high above Tomorrowland on the Astro Orbitor or join the gang in Monstropolis for the Monster's Inc. Laugh Floor.

☐ Help the monsters of Monstropolis at the Monster's Inc. Laugh Floor

> Mike and Sulley need your help to power Monstropolis. You will not want to miss this show full of fun to help the monsters meet their quota.

> Mike is your host as he introduces you to some new monsters, including his nephew.

Text a joke, and you may even hear your name during the show.

☐ Read the Monster's Inc. notices on the bulletin board during your wait for the laugh floor.

As you wait in the hallway for the laugh floor to open, spend some time reading the various notices on the bulletin board. From lost and found to scare reports, the monsters have been hard at work to make sure the factory runs smoothly, and there are enough laughs to go around for Monstropolis.

☐ Meet Stitch and his friends at the Stitch Intergalactic Meet and Greet

Within Tomorrowland, Stitch and his friends have set up a meet and greet at the Galactic Federation. Take some time to meet your favorite characters from this new Disney classic, *Lilo, and Stitch*.

☐ Help Buzz Lightyear save the galaxy from the evil Emperor Zurg on the Buzz Lightyear's Space Ranger Spin

Hop in your intergalactic space vehicle and help Buzz Lightyear stop the evil Emperor Zurg from stealing the crystalic fusion battery cells. Shoot the bad guys and rack up points as you travel through the universe, keeping one step ahead of Zurg.

- [ ] Relax on a tour of Tomorrowland on the Tomorrowland Transit Authority PeopleMover

    Take a tour of Tomorrowland in style as you board the Tomorrowland Transit Authority PeopleMover to take you on a tour of the attractions around you.

    Watch as guests save Planet Z from Zurg, watch people zoom through the galaxy on Space Mountain, pass by the Monster's Inc. Laugh Floor and Stitches Great escape, and you also lounge in total comfort.

- [ ] Visit the Walt Disney classic Carousel of Progress

    Another classic animatronic show is the Carousel of Progress. Go back to the turn of the century with an all-American family as you relive the inventions and lifestyle through the decades.

    The Carousel of Progress debuted at the 1964 World's Fair and Walt Disney spoke that this was his favorite attraction and wanted it to remain a permanent part of his theme parks.

    John and Rover take us from 1900, 1920, 1950 and the present day, showing how technology has changed the way we live and make our lives easier.

    The Carousel of Progress holds the record for being the longest-running stage show of all time.

☐ Listen to the voice of Uncle Orville in Carousel of Progress voiced by the man of a thousand voices, Mel Blanc

Throughout the Carousel of Progress, you will hear uncle Orville from somewhere in the house, but you never see him. If you listen very carefully, you will hear the familiar voice of character actor and voice-over artist Mel Blanc best known for being the voice of Bugs Bunny.

☐ Ride on a rocket through space on Space Mountain

Fly through the cosmos on this classic Disney attraction. One of the last attractions overseen by Walt Disney. He wanted guests to know the feeling of space flight within his theme parks.

Originally opening at Walt Disney World's Magic Kingdom in 1975, this attraction was operational for almost two years before opening at Disneyland in 1977.

☐ Fly high over Tomorrowland on the Astro Orbitor

The Astro Orbitor, opening in 1974 as a part of the Tomorrowland expansion, has been a favorite of guests wanting to fly high over the lands in their own rocket ship.

☐ Join your favorite characters in the Dance Party

> Get your groove on in Tomorrowland when you dance to the best music in the galaxy with your favorite Disney characters.
>
> The fun is always waiting for guests in Tomorrowland when you feel the beat and show off your dance moves.

☐ Meet Buzz Lightyear in Tomorrowland

> Buzz Lightyear is taking time off from protecting the galaxy, and he is waiting for you. Get an autograph and picture with this famous Space Ranger near the Buzz Lightyear Astro Blasters attraction.

☐ Ride in the big race of the Tomorrowland Speedway

> Jump into your racecar and drive along the Tomorrowland Speedway. This attraction opened with the Magic Kingdom in 1971 and has been a favorite of guests ever since.
>
> Be sure to join the race on your next visit to Tomorrowland.

☐ Watch the show at Cosmic Ray's Starlight Café

> Join the fun at Cosmic Ray's at let Ray serenade you with his intergalactic synthesizer. Ray plays every day at the Magic Kingdom while guests dine in comfort.

Epcot

Introduction

Epcot, the Experimental Porotype Community of Tomorrow, was the brainchild of founder Walt Disney. Disney wanted this area to be a functioning community, housing twenty-thousand residents, and supplying businesses in a circular community.

While Disney's vision was never realized, Epcot still grasped his concept of technology, keeping the attractions within this theme park on the cutting edge of current knowledge.

The crowning glory of Epcot is Spaceship Earth, a Geodesic sphere at the entrance to the theme park. While the attractions have changed, the theme has remained the same throughout the Future World area of the park.

Epcot would expand to include the World Showcase, allowing visitors to see the countries of the world while never leaving the United States.

At park opening, the World Showcase included the United Kingdom, Canada, France, Germany, Italy, China, Japan, and Mexico. The area would expand to include Morocco and Norway, and plans to include Brazil are coming in the future.

Future World East

- [ ] Take a photo with Spaceship Earth in the background

    The entrance of Epcot is framed with Spaceship Earth, the most recognizable structure at Walt Disney World, second only to Cinderella castle.

    Be sure to get a picture with this famous Geodesic sphere as your backdrop as you enter Epcot.

- [ ] Visit Spaceship Earth and explore the path of communication from the earliest man

    Join your narrator, Dame Judith Dench, as she takes you on a ride from the time of Neanderthal man showing how our communication has grown and evolve as you travel through the geodesic sphere.

    From the earliest cave paintings, we travel through the first universal language, then onto early writing.

    Travel then to Rome and through the Renaissance, where we see great artists leave their mark on the world.

This attraction is not only educational but a treat for the entire family.

- [ ] Enjoy the glowing path through Future World

    Once the sun goes down, enjoy a light show only found at Epcot. The ground beneath your feet glows with thousands of twinkling lights to illuminate your path.

    This spectacular light show appears every evening, so be sure to spend some time experiencing this hidden treasure of Future World.

- [ ] Ride on Test Track and build your own virtual vehicle and see how your design matches up with others

    Have you ever wondered what goes into the millions of cars that are produced in the world? Now is your chance to become a car designer as you build the vehicle of your dreams on Test Track.

    Once you have built your car, jump in, and take your new creation through its paces. Test the braking, handling, and road changes before heading outdoors to press the pedal to the floor and speed to 65 miles per hour.

    A little piece of trivia, Test Track has the distinction of being the fastest attraction in all of Walt Disney World with the 65 miles per hour speed.

☐ Check out the latest in automotive technology at Test Track

> Before you leave the world of automotive excellence, stop to review the latest cars in the showroom. From SUVs to sports cars and everything in between, you may just find the car of your dreams at Test Track.

☐ Study the history of space flight to the moon

> Outside the entrance of Mission Space, guests will find a giant statue of the moon with several markings. If you walk around this giant statue, you will find these markings representing the moon landings, crewed and uncrewed, that have been part of the history of our travels to space.

☐ Travel into space on Mission Space

> Have you ever wanted to become an astronaut and travel to the farthest reaches of space? Now is your chance as you don your space suit and leave the Earth to travel to the red planet, Mars. Mission Space is a high-intensity centrifuge that gives guests the experience of space travel.
>
> For those looking for a less intense experience, try the orbit around the earth on the green team without the motion but still getting the experience of space travel without space sickness.

☐ Continue your space training at the Advance Training Lab before you leave Mission Space

As you arrive back on earth, stop at the Advanced Training Lab to test your ability in team building tests or play through the Space Base. Before you are done, send an interplanetary postcard to your friends and family.

☐ Ride the Guardians of the Galaxy roller coaster

Become part of the Guardians of the Galaxy as you become one with the action in the latest roller coaster to grace Walt Disney World.

The new coaster will send you spinning through space to dodge obstacles while helping your favorite superheroes guard against the supervillains of the furthest stretches of space.

☐ Visit the Dreamers Point statue at Epcot

Walt Disney's vision was the beginning of everything you see throughout the Disney parks. Many guests have visited the Partners statue at the Magic Kingdom, and now guests will have a chance to see this great man with the newest statue to grace a Disney Park.

Stop to pay your respects to Walt Disney at the newest Dreamers Point statue coming soon to Epcot.

Future World West

☐ Visit your favorite Pixar characters at the Epcot Character Spot

Hidden away from the high-intensity rides and attractions of Epcot is a unique area that allows guests to come face to face with their favorite characters from Pixar films.

Meet Wreck-it Ralph and Vanellope from *Wreck-it Ralph* or Joy and Sadness from *Inside Out* in special themed areas. You may be surprised by the characters which may show up in this area from time to time.

Make new memories with these iconic characters during your time in Future World.

☐ Go on a journey with Nemo and his friends on The Seas with Nemo and Friends

Jump inside a clamshell and dive under the sea with Nemo and all his friends as you hunt for Nemo and Squirt with Marlin, Dory, and the entire cast of the Pixar hit movie *Finding Nemo*.

Avoid getting stung by jellyfish, hide from sharks in a shipwreck, and watch out for undersea mines to remain safe while hunting down the little fish.

Marvel at Nemo's friends as they interact with live fish in the 5.7 million-gallon fish tank.

☐ Spend some time chatting with Crush the turtle in Turtle Talk

Join your favorite one-hundred fifty-year-old turtle, Crush, in Turtle Talk. Watch as Crush interacts with your little ones live and in real-time. Crush will play games, tell jokes, and answer questions from the kids as he brings you his message from under the waves.

☐ Observe marine animals from all over the world in SeaBase

Boasting one of the largest fish tanks in the world, SeaBase gets guests up close and personal to exotic fish, dolphins, manatees, sharks, and a plethora of sea life in this interactive area of The Seas with Nemo and Friends.

Learn about sharks and how to stay safe in the ocean. Interact with the small tanks where you can find familiar clownfish, blue tangs, and the rest of your Finding Nemo friends.

Before you go, watch the gentle Manatees float in their happy home at SeaBase.

☐ Go on a journey through Living with the Land and see the future of growing our natural resources

In the Land pavilion in Future World, step into a boat and travel through the Living with the Land attraction to learn the latest agriculture. Listen as your narrator explains the history of farming and the latest innovations and growing techniques.

From hydroponics to sustainable fishing, Living with the Land offers guests a real-time tour of the future of the food on our table.

☐ Go on the Behind the Seeds tour in Living with the Land

While there are many tours offered throughout the theme parks of Walt Disney World, one of the lesser-known tours is the Behind the Seeds tour at the Living with the Land attraction.

Experts take small groups through the growing area, explaining the various growing techniques in great detail, allowing them to experience a whole new world of agriculture.

Spend time learning about sustainable fish farms and the history of the technological advancements of planting.

☐ Experience the tastes of Living with the Land

> All of the plants you watched growing right before your eyes are developed to supply the restaurants in Epcot. Living with the Land growing area produces over thirty tons of fruits and vegetables to provide guests with the freshest ingredients for their meal.
>
> Stop in at one of the restaurants in the Land or the Seas with Nemo and Friends to get your taste of the future.

☐ See Awesome Planet in the Land pavilion

> This ten-minute film takes guests on the greatest real estate sales pitch you will ever hear. Join Ty Burrell as he explains the virtue of our planet and sells you on this valuable piece of property.
>
> Do not miss this great sales pitch on your visit to the Land Pavilion at Epcot.

☐ Travel to the wonders of the world on Soarin' around the World

> Step inside the airplane hangar of Soarin' Around the World as this attraction takes guests on the greatest flight of their lives, traveling to the furthest reaches of their imagination.

Visit the pyramids at Giza, the Taj Mahal in India, and the Eiffel Tower in Paris.

Witness the natural wonders of the world like the Matterhorn in Switzerland, the Arctic ocean, Iguazu Falls in Argentina, and a herd of elephants in Africa.

End your flight at Epcot just in time for a spectacular fireworks display.

☐ Visit the open house and Journey into Imagination with Figment

Welcome to the open house of the Imagination Institute, where you can explore the five senses in a whole new way.

Watch out for the little purple dragon Figment as he tries to hijack the open house with his humorous way of seeing the world.

Celebrate imagination in this one of a kind open house.

☐ Spend some time with the gravity-defying waterfall at the Imagination Institute

Once you are back outdoors, you may think you are safely back on a planet where the laws of nature are constant. Not the case in front of the Imagination

Institute as you find gravity-defying fountains and a wall fall that falls up. Epcot engineers can bring the impossible to life in Future World.

☐ See the Disney and Pixar Short Film Festival

Guests can sit in comfort to watch some of the enchanting short subject films from Disney Animation and Pixar.

Stop during your hectic day, and enjoy these cartoons at Epcot.

☐ Visit Club Cool and taste sodas from around the world

Another lesser-known attraction at Epcot is Club Cool, an out of the way attraction that allows guests to taste soft drinks from all over the world.

Whether you like Krest ginger ale from Mozambique or Smart Watermelon from China, Club Cool has something from the four corners of the world.

Be sure to sample Beverly; this exotic flavor has become an internet sensation, taste Beverly and sees for yourself what all the excitement is about.

World Showcase

The World Showcase opened at Epcot on October 1, 1982, with nine countries represented around the man-made lake. The countries represented included Mexico, China, the United States, Germany, Italy, Japan, France, the United Kingdom, and Canada. 1984 brought Morocco and Norway would round out the countries in 1986.

Some of the countries imagined but never realized include Spain, Israel, and Africa.

The World Showcase offers guests a chance to see the architecture, crafts, food, characters and meet cast members from each country along their travels.

During the Epcot Flower and Garden Festival, guests can see topiaries as well as regional plants from all over the world. The Food and Wine Festival, one of the more popular festivals, offers guests flavors from every corner of the globe along with libations for every taste.

☐ Get the kid's artistic side flowing at the Kidcot stations in each country

Throughout the World Showcase, you will find Kidcot signs giving the little ones in your party an opportunity to decorate coloring pages themed to the eleven countries throughout World Showcase.

Get their passport stamped with individual stamps in each country to commemorate their time traveling the world.

Mexico

☐ Visit the Mexico pavilion and rediscover the world of Coco.

As you walk through the Mexico pavilion of the World Showcase, you can marvel at the ancient Aztec structure recreated at Epcot. As you step inside this temple, stop and read about the movie Coco and see the traditions of Día De Los Muertos. Miguel and his family, living a dead, greet you along with sugar skulls, dioramas, and skeletons that give you a sense of these century-old traditions.

Inside the pyramid, you can find the perfect souvenir at the traditional market and rest from your day at San Angel Inn with traditional Mexican food.

- ☐ Take a ride with the Three Caballeros on the Gran Fiesta Tour with the Three Caballeros

    Join in the fiesta at the Gran Fiesta Tour with the Three Caballeros. Donald is enjoying his vacation as he cliff dives, shops, and celebrates with the native people in this grand tour of Mexico. Celebrate Cinco de Mayo or Dia de Los Muertos before coming back to Orlando.

- ☐ Enjoy high-end Tequila at La Cava de Tequila

    A lesser-known area within the Mexico pavilion is La Cava de Tequila, a small tequila bar offering the best libations since 2009. Sample offerings from the best international distilleries or tequila pairings to accompany your meal at San Angel Inn Restaurante.

    During the food and wine festival, this small bar boasts some of the longest lines in the World Showcase as guests make their way to the Mexico pavilion for their favorite agave flavors.

- ☐ Visit with Donald Duck in his traditional Hispanic attire

    Donald Duck, one of the fab five, has come to Mexico to greet guests in his traditional Mexican sarape and sombrero. Donald visits with guests throughout the day, signing autographs and getting photos. Do not miss this great opportunity to visit with your favorite Disney duck.

- [ ] Spend time with Mariachi Cobre at the Mexico pavilion

    This 12-piece traditional Mariachi group has been performing for amazed crowds at Epcot for many years.

    Established in 1971, this small group of musicians performed locally before holding auditions to expand their sound. Mariachi Cobre began performing internationally and became one of the leading performing groups in the world.

    Relocating to Florida, guests of the World Showcase now have a fantastic opportunity to hear this award-winning troupe perform daily.

Norway

- [ ] Visit an authentic Norway church and see Norwegian artifacts

    Enter the Stave church and discover this hidden treasure in the Norway pavilion. Inside this traditional Stave church, you will get a glimpse into the history and culture of this proud country.

From arts and crafts, clothing style, and Nors history, you will come away from this little church with a newfound love of Norway.

☐ Come face to face with Nors Vikings

As you spend some time in the Norway pavilion, be careful, or you just may find yourself battling real Vikings. These fierce warriors can be found walking the streets, waiting for unsuspecting guests to pose for pictures.

☐ Find real grass on the roof of KringlaBakeriogKafe

The bakery within the Norway pavilion has a well-kept secret just above the heads of guests exploring this quaint area of the World Showcase. If you look closely, you will notice there is real grass growing atop the roof of this store.

This traditional type of sod roof has been used for hundreds of years by Norway's residents as the sod offers excellent insulation during the cold winter months. There are competitions in some communities for the best roofs.

☐ Enjoy a traditional Norway treat at KringlaBakeriogKafe

For guests looking for a snack during their time in Norway, stop off at the KringlaBakeriogKafe. Whether you want a sweet Troll Horn or Sven's

Green Apple Cheesecake, there is something for everyone to try. For something on the savory side, try a Ham and Apple sandwich or Norwegian club sandwich.

No matter your preference, there is something you will love at KringlaBakeriogKafe.

☐ Go on a journey with Anna, Elsa, Olaf, and all their friends on Frozen Ever After

Wander through Arendelle just in time for the summer festival. Wander through Oakens to find those big summer blowouts before boarding a traditional Nors sailing vessel and taking off to find Anna, Elsa, and all their friends.

Watch Olaf sing and dance in the frozen wilderness, listen to grandfather Pabbie share the stories with the smaller trolls before coming to Queen Elsa ice palace to hear her sing.

Finally, you will find Anna and Elsa as they celebrate together.

☐ Meet Queen Elsa and Princess Anna at Sommerhas

Queen Elsa and Princess Anna are in residence at the Norway pavilion and are waiting for the honor of meeting you on your next trip to Epcot. Spend some time with these royal sisters and get two more famous signatures for your autograph book with Anna and Elsa at Sommerhas.

China

- [ ] Stand in the center of the temple in China

    The scale building, an exact copy of the Temple of Heaven in Bejing is so structurally sound, and if guests stand in the direct center of this temple and speak normally, they will be surprised that they hear their voice echoing back to them from above.

    This acoustically perfect structure is a truly unique experience at the World Showcase.

- [ ] Meet Mulan at the Temple of Heaven building

    One of your favorite characters has stepped right out of Disney animation and into the China pavilion. Mulan greets guests for photo opportunities and autographs throughout the day.

    Do not miss this opportunity to meet one of your favorite Disney characters.

- [ ] Experience the Reflections of China in circle vision

    Spend some time experiencing the sights, sounds, and people of China in this 360-degree film showing guests the history and industry of this mysterious land.

Join the poet as he narrates the sights of the Great Wall of China, the Forbidden City, Shanghai, Hong Kong, and Beijing. This ancient land embraces traditions held for thousands of years with the technology and innovation of the bustling city.

Spend some time with the people of China during your visit to the China Pavilion at Epcot.

☐ Find an exotic souvenir within the shops of the China Pavilion

Throughout the narrow streets within the China pavilion at the World Showcase, you will find walls lined with authentic Chinese toys and collectibles. From jade sculptures to hand-painted silk fans, clothing to handbags, you will find everything on your list.

Ask one of the artists to hand-paint your name on a hand fan in Chinese script for a truly one of a kind collectible.

☐ Indulge your love of authentic Chinese food at the Nine Dragons

Dine in the opulence of Chinese décor as you savor cuisine from the orient. Ornate carvings and traditional paper lanterns adorn this restaurant as diners enjoy exquisite meals prepared by the best chefs from China.

Make your reservation today to enjoy the delicacies of the China pavilion.

- [ ] Visit the refreshment outpost as you travel through the World Showcase

    As you work your way through the World Showcase, you will find a small area between China and Germany with several huts and refreshments.

    While very little is known about this area, the rumors state that, during the development of the World Showcase, Disney entered into negotiations with several African nations to create a pavilion to bring this beautiful continent to Epcot. This area was believed to be a placeholder, but the area was never developed.

    While the details of whether this area was to be used for an African country are cloudy, this rest stop remains for guests to take a well-deserved breather along their travels.

- [ ] Spend some time with the artisans making handcrafted gifts

    Throughout the day, you will find artisans creating some of the most beautiful items you will find at Epcot.

Watch artists hand carve animals before your eyes or stop off at the face painting booth to become a new character or one of your favorite animals.

☐ Explore the international Coca Cola™ items in the Outpost

You may have noticed throughout your visit to Walt Disney World that Coca Cola™ products and symbols are a part of the resort.

This holds true in the Outpost, where you can purchase a refreshing drink on your way to the next country. If you look around this area, you will find several crates with the Coca Cola™ name in various languages waiting to be shipped to thirsty patrons throughout the world. Antique vending machines are scattered around this area also, a reminder of days gone by.

Germany

☐ Enjoy the model trains and the countryside of Germany

As you come upon the Germany pavilion in the World Showcase, guests will find a charming miniature landscape with train tracks winding their way throughout. The model trains travel through the towns and countryside, delivering their cargo to the country of Germany.

One Hundred Things to do at Walt Disney World Before you Die

- [ ] Visit with Snow White and the Seven Dwarfs

    The first Disney princess, Snow White, poses for pictures and signs autographs for adoring fans throughout the day at the Germany pavilion in the World Showcase.

    Snow White, a traditional German folk tale written by the Brothers Grimm in 1812, was adopted by the Disney filmmakers and brought to the big screen in 1937.

    Now she comes to life with her friends to create special moments daily.

- [ ] Indulge your sweet tooth at Karamell-Kuche

    Sponsored by Werther's Original, guests can purchase their favorite caramel candy in this quaint shop. Let your imagination run wild when you sample caramel popcorn, apples, and strawberries. Purchase your favorites bags to take with you as you continue your exploration of the countries of the world.

- [ ] Find the perfect ornament for your Christmas tree in Glas Und Porzellen

    Handcrafted ornaments abound in this tiny shop. Find your favorite new ornament to display on your

Christmas tree as a remembrance of your time at the Germany pavilion.

Everything from hand-blown Disney themed ornaments to the traditional pickle ornaments can be found.

Imagine the joy you will feel each year as you carefully unwrap this beautiful memory.

☐ Dine at Biergarten and listen to an authentic Oompah band

Are you looking for a hearty meal to keep you going on your journey through the World Showcase? Make reservations at Biergarten!

Meet new friends as you sit at tables with other guests in the park. Your wait staff greets you in traditional German costumes and offer a variety of beers and wines from every region of Germany.

Authentic German food greets you as you indulge in Bratwurst, Sauerkraut, carved meats, traditional salads, and apple strudel. Sample a little or satisfy your cravings as you spend time savoring every offering.

During your meal, listen to an authentic Oompah band playing songs passed down from generation to generation. Dance and sing along as these talented musicians entertain you during your meal.

☐ Discover the history of German folklore in the courtyard at the Germany pavilion

As you stand near the fountain in the courtyard of the German pavilion, look above your head at the statue of St. George slaying a dragon. This statue brings German history to Florida as guests can learn about this 11th-century legend.

Italy

☐ Sip authentic Italian wine in the Italy Pavilion

For the wine lovers, be sure to visit Tutto Gusto Winery to taste old favorites and new vintage wines. Throughout the year, this small shop offers guests the latest flavors to tempt even the best wine experts.

Be sure to stop by for a glass of wine on your next visit to the Italy pavilion.

☐ Watch the living statuary in Italy

Visitors to Italy marvel each year at the historic sculpture that has been a regular part of the landscape of this beautiful country. Walt Disney World brings this tradition to Epcot in a whole new way.

Throughout the day, you may notice Statues appear and disappear before your eyes. These talented performers give guests a thrill to see details statues move imperceptibly in the courtyard of this pavilion.

Enjoy the traditional artwork of Italy in a new and different way.

☐ Dine in Italian opulence at Tutto Italia Ristorante

Old world charm meets fine Italian cuisine at this appealing restaurant within the Italy pavilion. Sample traditional pasta dishes and delectable pizzas as you relax in this elegant setting. Sample wines paired perfectly with your meal as you take a breather from your busy day.

The American Adventure

☐ Experience the Spirit of Liberty singers

Within the American Adventure building, you can marvel at the architecture within. Still, the true beauty of this room can be found when the Spirit of Liberty singers stand in the center of this room to bring the sounds of America to the guests. Listen to the perfect harmony of this singing group as they bring the songs to life that built the country from the earliest days of the first settlers.

Each era is represented in song as their voices lift the patriotism of every American.

☐ Explore the American Adventure artwork

Throughout this building, guests can admire the vast works of art that Disney artists have contributed to this experience.

Enormous oil paintings depicting moments in history line the walls. Even the furnishings are exact reproductions of classic styles that have sat in the homes of our founding fathers. Be sure to take some time to marvel at the talent of these amazing artists.

☐ Watch as Benjamin Franklin, and Mark Twain take you through the history of the United States of America in The American Adventure

Settle in and watch as Benjamin Franklin and Mark Twain bring the history of the United States back to life in this dramatic stage production.

Revisit the origins of the first settlers as they began creating a new history in this strange land. Watch the struggles, hopes, fears, and victories as they show guests the timeline that built this amazing country.

Meet historical figures that sacrificed their lives to moving us out of stagnation and into new ways of thinking. Celebrate the inventions that made

America the leader in innovations throughout the world.

You will leave with renewed pride in this nation as you watch The American Experience.

☐ Listen to your favorite artists on stage at The American Garden

The main stage of the American Adventure is the focal point of this pavilion. Throughout the year, you will find your favorite musicians entertaining guests with songs from every era.

Plan some time to hear your favorite bands like Rick Springfield, The Village People, Survivor, Foghat, or Lonestar. Enjoy the classic songs from your favorite Disney films as Walt Disney World artists bring enjoyments with songs from *Aladdin*, *The Little Mermaid,* and *Tarzan*.

Do not miss out on this intimate stage to hear the songs you love.

☐ Watch the Fife and Drum corps perform

As you stroll through the American Adventure, you can be transported back in time to hear the strains of a real Fife and Drum Corps as they march through the pavilion. This precision team, made up of musicians at the top of their field, demonstrates the music that could be heard during the revolutionary war. Watch as these talented musicians demonstrate the marching patterns that would have been seen during parades and military demonstrations.

Keep a lookout for the Fife and Drum Corps on your next trip to the American Adventure.

Japan

☐ Listen to the Matsuriza Taiko drummer's performance at the pagoda in Japan

For over two-thousand years, the Matsuriza Taiko drummers have performed during religious ceremonies, festivals, and battlefields. Now, the World Showcase brings these talented performers to the Japan pavilion to perform for you.

Throughout the day, watch as these musicians stand in front of a traditional Japanese pagoda and demonstrate the precision historical drumming of thousands of years.

☐ Discover the secret of the Japanese pagoda

The tall, imposing structure standing at the front of the Japan pavilion holds a secret known only to those familiar with these Pagodas.

Each level of the structure is designed to honor the five elements—Earth, Water, Fire, Wind, and Space. Stop at the base of the Pagoda to marvel at this beautifully constructed building.

☐ Shop for authentic Japanese treasures

Within the shops of the Japan pavilion, you will find authentic treasures from the orient. Everything from traditional toys to jewelry to clothing can be found in these shops.

Find new additions to your home décor as you find a Japanese tea set, chopsticks, and wall hangings. Find something for the kids as they pick out their new favorite toy.

☐ Get a pearl straight from the oyster

For those guests looking for the unusual souvenir, stop off in the Japan pavilion to pick a pearl from live oysters straight from the tank.

Within the shops, you can take your time to pick an oyster and watch it opened right before your eyes. Let the pearl experts' size and weigh your new treasure then give you options to mount your new jewel in the perfect setting. Whether you prefer a necklace, ring, or earrings, you can find your new favorite piece of jewelry in the Japan pavilion at the World Showcase.

One Hundred Things to do at Walt Disney World Before you Die

Morocco

☐ Dine on authentic Moroccan food at Restaurant Marrakesh

> Dine at Restaurant Marrakesh for an authentic Moroccan meal
>
> Find a truly unique dining experience within the World Showcase as you dine on delicacies like shish kebab, couscous, roasted meats, and traditional desserts. Bask in the glow of stained-glass lanterns as the staff serve your every need.
>
> Enjoy the hospitality of the Moroccan people as you enjoy this once in a lifetime experience.

☐ Walk through the streets of Marrakesh and shop for wonders from the east

> Throughout the narrow streets of the Morocco pavilion, the shop overflow with treasures from the east. Take your time to find just the right reminder of your time in Morocco, whether you fancy clothing, artwork, or jewelry.
>
> Handmade bracelets, earrings, and necklaces dazzle the eyes. Find an authentic dress or shirt from various hand-made designs. Hand-painted artwork or glassware can be found all over this magical land.

☐ Meet with Aladdin and Jasmine on the streets of Morocco

Meet with Princess Jasmine and her love, Aladdin, as they greet guests throughout the day in Morocco. Dressed in her royal finest, Jasmine will grace your photos along with Aladdin in his purple vest and traditional pants.

Do not miss this royal couple as they offer a great picture during your time in the World Showcase.

☐ Marvel at the architecture of Morocco

Throughout the Morocco pavilion, guests are transported to this magical land. Detailed columns and archways rise to create stunning visuals. Walk into a courtyard glittering with colorful mosaics. Artisans have spent thousands of hours painstakingly creating these visuals for guests to enjoy. Spend some time drinking in the exquisite beauty of the architecture of Morocco.

☐ Learn the history and customs of Morocco

Hidden in the Morocco pavilion is a gem overlooked by many guests visiting Epcot. The gallery of arts and history provides guests with a glimpse into the customs and history surrounding this land.

See the traditional garments surviving thousands of years of history. Body art and jewelry give guests a representation of aesthetics. Fantasia, a traditional costume for rider and horse, are currently on display.

Do not miss this beautiful gem within the Morocco pavilion.

☐ Find the Tower of Terror framed in the Morocco pavilion

Guests may tour the Morocco pavilion without ever noticing that one of the tallest structures you see is, in fact, the back of the Tower of Terror attraction at Disney Hollywood Studios.

Since this structure was tall enough to be seen from Epcot, the Imagineers decided to create the back view to blend with the buildings of the Morocco pavilion.

France

☐ Sip French wine and champagne

Synonymous with France is a tradition of French wine and champagne. Now is your opportunity to sample these amazing vintages in an authentic setting in the France pavilion.

Whether your taste leans towards the sweet, bubbly wines or drier red wines, you can find your new favorite along the street of France.

- [ ] Find delicious sweets on the streets of France

    French pastries are known all over the world for its delicacies, and now you have the chance to sample these offerings on the streets of France. Try a handmade chocolate dessert or ice cream to satisfy your sweet tooth. Take home a box of your favorite truffles to savor long after your time at Walt Disney World is over.

    Sweets to satisfy every visitor can be found in France.

- [ ] Watch Impressions De France and be transported to the beauty of the French countryside

    Settle back to visit France as the World Showcase brings this enchanted land to Epcot. Visit the cliffs of Normandy, join in the harvest at the wineries, and travel via railway through the pastoral countryside.

    Enjoy the excitement of Paris as you walk the Champs-Elysees, Notre Dame, the Seine, and the Eiffel Tower. As you enjoy the sights of France, listen to the lilting music of French composers as they complete this immersive experience.

☐ Watch the Beauty and the Beast Sing-Along

> Join narrator Angela Lansbury as you watch this new retelling of the Disney classic *Beauty and the Beast*. You will be swept away with your favorite songs and characters as you relive this tale.
>
> Before your time with Belle and the Beast are through, you will be carried away where they live happily ever after.

☐ Find your new fragrance in the perfume shops of France

> Sights and sounds are not the only ways to experience this great country. Within the Plume et Palette in the France pavilion, French perfume designers display their latest scents for the enjoyment of guests as they sample a variety of aromas for every occasion.
>
> From the origins of Coco Chanel to the newest scents, guests can find the perfect cologne to accent their lives within the Plume et Palette.

☐ Find your favorite Disney characters from French stories

> French fairytales have been the mainstay of your favorite Disney films. Within the streets of the France pavilion, guests can meet these characters for a magical souvenir. Throughout the day, Aurora

from *Sleeping Beauty* can be seen interacting with children and adults. Belle and Beast are also seen taking photos and signing autographs, and Cinderella enchants guests in her ballgown.

Do not miss your chance to meet these classic characters while visiting France at the World Showcase.

☐ Watch French street performers during the Epcot Food and Wine Festival

Each October, the International Food and Wine Festival takes over Epcot. Within the France pavilion, you can find the most exceptional talent direct from France along the streets of this tiny pavilion.

Jugglers, stilt walkers, dancers, and clowns greet guests while dazzling them with their talents. Be sure to spend some time with these artists during the International Food and Wine Festival.

☐ Ride on Remy's Ratatouille Adventure

Remy is once again in the kitchen, and you can go along to see his adventures from the perspective of a rat.

Walk across the rooftops of Paris before you hop aboard your ratmobile. Ride along this trackless dark ride as you dart beneath the counters and hide among the food in the pantry to escape from the newest threat.

Join Remy and his friends coming soon

United Kingdom

☐ Listen to the sounds of the British Revolution in the garden of the United Kingdom

British bands have been the backbone of the rock and roll scene for decades, and now guests can enjoy the sounds of their favorite rock bands with the British Revolution performing at the United Kingdom pavilion.

Performing daily, this talented group recreates hit songs from The Beatles, the Rolling Stones, Queen, The Who, and many more.

Framed in this charming garden, guests can settle in to enjoy their favorite songs from every era.

Sing along or dance to these hits as you get a taste of the pioneers of modern rock and roll.

☐ Find your favorite themed merchandise in the Toy Soldier

> Along the cobblestone streets of the United Kingdom pavilion, guests can enter the Toy Soldier and find the best in English merchandise. Hats, T-shirts, books, and toys from your favorite bands and shows can be found within this shop. Doctor Who, The Who, The Rolling Stones, and David Bowie can be found to add to your collections.

☐ Enjoy a traditional meal and a pint at the Rose and Crown Pub

> For those who enjoy the tastes of the United Kingdom, this is your chance to get authentic fair at the Rose and Crown Pub. Whether you enjoy fish and chips or bangers and mash, you can find your favorite. Are you looking for an adult beverage? Get a pint of your favorite beer to go along with your meal. Do not miss this chance to satisfy your hunger at the Rose and Crown pub.

☐ Enjoy the details of the United Kingdom Pavilion

> Within all of the World Showcase, Walt Disney World Imagineers have worked tirelessly to immerse guests in the wonder of the countries of the world. Within the United Kingdom Pavilion, the level of detail is no different. Stop for a moment to look at the rooftops and notice the blackened chimneys

from years of fireplace use. Plants and flowers in intricate designs in the garden areas are a feast for the eyes and nose.

Be sure to enjoy the wonder of detail around you throughout the United Kingdom Pavilion.

Canada

☐ See the wonder of Canada in Canada Far and Wide

Join your host as he takes you on a whirlwind tour of Canada in this show featured in the Canada pavilion.

The countryside comes alive through the sites, traditions, and famous people that come from the country to the north of the United States.

Found in the cool mountains within this pavilion, spend some time learning about this lovely country in the Canada theater.

☐ See authentic Canadian totem poles

As you walk into the Canada pavilion, towering high above the rest of the pavilions are the three totem poles at the entrance. The totem with the eagle was installed and tells the story of a boy who finds an eagle in fishnet and releases the bird. Years later, when the tribe is struggling to find food, the boy goes to the shore and find this same eagle has brought food to repay the boy's kindness.

The two totems you find nearby are relatively new, installed in 2017, and bring further traditional artwork to the pavilion for guests to enjoy.

☐ Get amazing photos at the hidden waterfall

Through the enormous rock formations in the Canada pavilion, guests are amazed as they come from a cascading waterfall hidden in the back of this area.

Take one of a kind pictures of your time at the World Showcase on the rocks with streaming natural water flowing in the background. Watch as the water fills the stream that flows throughout this rustic recreation of Canada.

☐ Visit the Butchart Garden area in Canada

The highlight of your time in the Canada pavilion can be found strolling through the recreation of Butchart Garden found in Victoria.

With flowers from every region designed to enchant guests, the sights and smells are truly amazing. The water formation completes the pictures framed by the delicate blooms throughout Butchart Gardens.

☐ Visit Northwest Mercantile for all your cold-weather needs

The Northwest Mercantile offers guests the best that Canada has to offer. From clothing, toys, and collectibles, this outpost on the northern tundra is a shoppers dream when visiting the Canada pavilion.

Epcot Flower and Garden Festival

☐ Spend time with the topiaries throughout the Flower and Garden Festival

From the moment you walk through the gates of Epcot, you will be amazed by the talented artist's creations in topiaries. Plants and flowers are designed to represent your favorite Disney characters. From Mickey Mouse, Minnie Mouse, Donald Duck, and Goofy, you will fall in love with the artistry of these topiaries.

☐ Visit your favorite rock bands at the American Gardens Theater

During this magical time at the Flower and Garden Festival, your favorite bands from every era bring their hit songs to life. Check the calendar to make sure to see your favorite musical artists during this event.

☐ Get ready for new recipes and taste flavors in the World Showcase

> Recently, the Flower and Garden Festival has brought new booths alongside the flower and garden to combine the Food and Wine Festival with this springtime event.
>
> Throughout the Future World area of the park, you may find cooking demonstrations along with wine pairings to your favorite meals.
>
> Walk along the World Showcase and visit the booths set up with delicacies from every nation. Sights and scents combine with taste to bring this event to a whole new level.

Epcot International Food and Wine Festival

☐ Learn new recipes from your favorite celebrity chefs

> Throughout the years, Epcot has featured celebrity chefs from your favorite televisions shows to host demonstrations of their signature dishes.
>
> Carla Hall from The Chew, Buddy Valastro from Cake Boss, Stuart O'Keeffe of Celebrity Chefs of Beverly Hills, Jamie Deen from Road Tasted, and many many more offer guests once in a lifetime

☐ Get custom Food and Wine Festival merchandise throughout the event

Each year, Disney designers create a variety of themed souvenirs just in time for the event. Stop off at the specialty store to get everything from cookbooks to aprons, cutting boards to wine glasses as a remembrance of this special time.

☐ Purchase a Drink pass for the World Showcase

Throughout the World Showcase, guests can sample drinks from every country. While each booth takes cash and credit cards, some guests opt to purchase a drink card that allows for up to eight cocktails at a discount from the on-site prices.

In addition to discounts, this drink pass allows guests to speed through the ordering process to keep their day free for traveling through the pavilions.

☐ Sample delicacies from around the world

Eleven countries comprise the World Showcase, but during the Epcot International Food and Wine Festival, guests can indulge with flavors from the four corners of the world.

Try tastes from Greece, India, Ireland, or New Zealand from savory offerings to the sweets enjoyed by locals in these regions.

Disney's Animal Kingdom

Introduction

The fourth theme park opened at Walt Disney World on Earth Day 1998. The Disney Animal Kingdom celebrated its opening with a huge opening ceremony that would include larger than life animal floats, dancers, and dignitaries, including famed primatologist Jane Goodall.

Disney Animal Kingdom began with the Kilimanjaro Safari as well as It's Tough to be a Bug and DINOSAUR. Guests could enjoy Conservation Station, where families could learn about the importance of the earth.

The exploration trails offered guests an up-close opportunity to see wild animals in native habitats while Dinoland U.S.A. gave guests a glimpse into the past.

The years following the opening offered new exciting attractions like Kali River Rapids and Expedition Everest.

Now, guests can go to the world of Pandora in addition to the classic attractions.

Discovery Island

☐ Visit with exotic animals as you enter Disney's Animal Kingdom

As you begin your adventure at Disney's Animal Kingdom, the experience starts as you walk through the gates. Cast members, holding Madagascar hissing cockroaches or cases with snakes from exotic regions, can be viewed in safety and security by these expert animal handlers.

Before running off to this excitement of the theme park, stop to admire these amazing creatures.

☐ Find DiVine

Guests walking through the entrance to Disney's Animal Kingdom may notice the wide variety of plants surrounding them but never think that one may be looking back. DiVine is a Disney's Animal Kingdom performer that stilt walks dressed as the vines and leaves of the surroundings.

You may walk right by this talented performer, but once DiVine starts walking among you, it is impossible to look away.

- [ ] Take pictures of the animal sculptures on the Tree of Life

The centerpiece to Disney's Animal Kingdom standing in the center of this majestic park. The Tree of Life brings life to the Animal Kingdom, giving a backdrop to thousands of photographs taken by the guests entering the theme park.

This representation of the Baobob tree stands one-hundred forty-five feet and boasts over three hundred animal carvings. If you stand at the picture spots throughout the park, you can see the detailed sculptures, including a whale, gorilla, eagle, horse, tiger, lion, and many many more.

- [ ] Visit the queue for It's Tough to be a Bug and see some of the Tree of Life up close

Beneath the fifty-foot base of the Tree of Life, guests can enter the queue for It's Tough to be a Bug, an animatronic video show.

While in the queue, take a look at the roots of this magnificent tree, and you will get up close and personal with every kind of animal from pterodactyls, orangutan, and elephant. Do not miss this chance to view the Tree of Life carvings from a new perspective.

☐ Read the posters for the greatest bug musicals of all time

While waiting for the show to begin, stop to read some of the posters around the underground world you find yourself in. Posters from Antie describe the amazing abilities of ants. Beauty and the Bees give guests a glimpse into the way bees make honey, Barefoot in the Bark helps guests understand termites a little bit better.

Do not miss the advertisements for these upcoming shows in the bug world.

☐ Put on your bug eyes and become an honorary bug in It's Tough to be a Bug

When the doors open, you and your party get to become honorary bugs. Join your host Flik from *A Bug's Life* as he walks you through the life of the millions of bugs throughout the world.

Keep a sharp eye out for Hopper as he tries to punish you for invading their world. Before your time in the bug world is done, take new respect of the insect world with you as you continue your day.

☐ Join Russell and Dug to become a Wilderness Explorer

Russell has taken up residence to recruit small guests to become Wilderness Explorers at Disney's Animal Kingdom. Pick up your guide map and start earning badges as you work your way through the park.

Do not forget to get a picture with your favorite Wilderness Explorer and his beloved furry pal, Dug.

☐ Find the perfect souvenir from your trip at Island Mercantile

The Island Mercantile offers guests a huge variety of items specialized to the Animal Kingdom park. From clothing to toys to décor, the Island Mercantile has the perfect something to proudly display from your time in the wild.

Pandora – The World of Avatar

☐ Touch the Flaska Reclinata

At the entrance to Pandora, you may notice a large plant reclining out into the pathway. This exotic plant offers guests their first chance to interact with this strange and wonderful land.

Touch the center of the Flaska Reclinata and watch as the plant comes to life and sprays a fine mist over the guests. These plants offer life-giving nourishment for those who pause to provide something in return.

☐ Become a musician as you pound the drums in the drum circle

As your exploration of Pandora continues, stop at the drum circle to learn the sounds of the Na'Vi. You may be surprised by the sounds around you. Instead of coming from beneath the drum head, you may find the sounds coming from overhead or behind you.

Do not forget to shake some of the gourds for a surprising new sound.

Throughout the day, stop to listen to the drum masters entertain you.

☐ Bask in the wonder of the floating mountains

The landscape of Pandora is the highlight of any visit to Disney's Animal Kingdom. As you stand below, be amazed at these solid rocks that defy gravity and offer wildlife a secure location to thrive in this extraordinary setting.

☐ Find the Sting bats on the floating mountains

The floating mountains are the centerpiece of Pandora, but hidden in the nooks are some of the wildlife of Pandora.

While in the queue for Avatar, Flights of Passage, you can get a glimpse of these elusive bats hanging on the floating mountains. While difficult to see, once you find them, you can be amazed by the multitude of animals hidden around you.

☐ Find the force perspective waterfalls

Throughout Pandora, life thrives in this mystical setting. High above in the hills, you will see movement along the top of this area. You may notice very small waterfalls moving in the distance. If you zoom in on these waterfalls with your camera, you will find that these are not waterfalls at all.

The Imagineers have created these areas with wheels that recreate falling water with mesh to represent the mist at the base of the falls.

☐ Find the Na'Vi footprints outside the Na'Vi River Journey

You will find hints throughout Pandora of the culture living in this amazing place. Outside the Na'Vi River Journey, the residents of Pandora have left their footprints behind. Before you enter the queue for this ride, stop and compare your foot to the large footprints you see. You can even find the prints of a child left behind.

☐ Explore the jungle on Na'Vi River Journey

Float down a lazy river as you become part of the life that flourishes in this jungle setting—Marvel at the bioluminescent plants surrounding the river. Animals watch from the riverbank to see the new people settling in the jungle.

Watch as the Na'Vi shaman greets you with a song as you float by and become part of the Na'Vi tribe.

- [ ] Explore the ruins in the Flights of Passage queue

    Earthlings came to this peaceful jungle in search of valuables but failed in their mission. Now you can walk through the remains of their base camp as you walk towards the Flights of Passage loading area.

    Notice small details throughout as to the people who came here before you. Notice the corrugated metal with the date of James Cameron's birthday.

    Enter the lab where scientists examine the wildlife of Pandora, big and small. Stop and explore the details of this long since abandoned outpost.

- [ ] Soar like an eagle on Avatar Flights of Passage

    Find your perfect avatar and jump on the back of a Banshee as you soar over the landscape of Pandora. Discover the wildlife and scenery as you feel the wind in your face. Travel to the shore and play in the waves before traveling to the treetops of the floating mountains.

    Feel your banshee breathe beneath you as you find the bioluminescence in the caves of Pandora.

☐ Find the handprint of James Cameron in the exit of Flights of Passage

One final secret can be found as you are leaving the Avatar Flights of Passage attraction. Director James Cameron, Producer Jon Landau and Jon Rohde Imagineer of Pandora have left their handprints behind as a symbol to the journey of the Avatar franchise. Following the traditions of the Na'Vi, these talented men have left their mark on this attraction.

☐ Get something to eat in the abandoned RDA structure

Throughout Pandora, you will find buildings left over from the occupation of the RDA. Now, guests can get a bite to eat in the commissary and see pictures of the troops that have long since left Pandora.

Enjoy a meal or grab a snack in this military building before continuing your exploration of Disney's Animal Kingdom.

☐ Pick a Banshee as your new pet

The world of Avatar can be brought home with you as you pick your new pet from the baby Banshees. These adorable Banshees are completely interactive, sitting atop your shoulder and moving to respond to the world around them.

Find your new best friend among the Banshees today.

Africa

- [ ] Join in the singing and dancing of Festival of the Lion King

    Sit in this round theater as you listen to the songs of the Disney classic, *The Lion King*. Timon, Pumba, Simba, and all of their friends welcome you as they bring the jungle to life once again.

    Watch as the monkeys entertain you with their gymnastics. Elegant birds dance in the center of the theater before Scar, and his minions take over the stage.

    This is a show you will not want to miss during your stay in the jungles of Disney's Animal Kingdom.

- [ ] Stop to enjoy the Tam Tam Drummers of Harambe

    Entertainment can be found throughout Africa, but the Tam Tam drummers are one of the most exciting groups in Disney's Animal Kingdom. This talented group brings the sounds of Africa to life as they interact with the guests and get them right in the middle of the action.

Stop during your travels to visit the locals to admire their talents.

- [ ] Travel through the African Savannah on the Kilimanjaro Safari

    The premier attraction in Africa is the Kilimanjaro Safari. Board a transport to take you on a grand tour of the African savannah with the wildlife on full display.

    Giraffe that walk along the roadways to greet guests, lions perched high above the savannah, cheetahs lounge in the shade of the trees while elephants feed and care for their young ones.

    Deadly alligators lay beneath the roadway and hippos lounge in the cool water.

    Do not miss this opportunity to see your favorite animals in their natural habitat at the Kilimanjaro Safari.

- [ ] Take the Safari tour in the evening to see the animals after dark

    During the summer months, Kilimanjaro Safari offers guests evening and nighttime tours to see the animals in their nocturnal setting. Most of the animals on the savannah sleep during the warmest part of the day, so guests will see them moving through their habitats in a whole new way.

Do not miss this opportunity to explore the wild like never before.

☐ Travel the Gorilla Falls Exploration Trail

Another way to get up close to these jungle animals is to explore the Gorilla Falls Exploration Trail just outside the Kilimanjaro Safari.

Take your time strolling through the tree-covered paths as you come across dozens of species of exotic birds. See the Hippopotamus beneath the water as they rest the day away under the water.

Watch as the gorilla care for their young and interact with the guests. Sometimes it is difficult to know who is observing who through the glass.

Take some time to learn about these exotic creatures with fascinating education centers throughout the pathways.

☐ Visit the street performers of Harambe

During your time in Harambe, you may hear the strains of instruments playing. Talented performers will be out on the streets, entertaining guests throughout their day. Kora TingaTinga is a Mandinka harp with a long, hardwood neck. Watch the Burudika comprised of talented musicians playing modern versions of traditional African music.

Do not miss these fantastic artists throughout Harambe at Disney's Animal Kingdom.

☐ Join Donald Duck at Tusker House restaurant

The Tucker House buffet offers a wide variety of delicacies for the entire family. While the food and décor keep guests coming back year after year, the real entertainment comes when Donald Duck joins in the fun to greet his guests, young and old.

Dine-in African opulence and interact with your favorite crazy duck in this fun and yummy experience.

Asia

☐ Watch the amazing birds of the UP! A Great Bird Adventure show

Join Russell and Dug as they bring this new show to the Animal Kingdom, starring exotic birds from around the world.

Watch as these birds show off their amazing abilities with the help of their loving trainers to earn their Wilderness Explorer badges.

☐ Dine at the Yak and Yeti in Asia

One of the best restaurants at Disney's Animal Kingdom is available at the Yak and Yeti, an upscale dining experience offering a wide variety of foods from Asia.

Savor shrimp lo mein or seared miso salmon. Enjoy Korean BBQ ribs or a Kobe beef burger.

For those looking for a cocktail, the bartenders offer thirst-quenching libations.

☐ Find the Prayer Tree in Asia

> As guests explore the Asia area of Disney's Animal Kingdom, you will notice a huge tree with hundreds of scarves tied to its branches. This is a traditional prayer tree to honor lost loved ones.

☐ Be amazed by the Tigers and other native animals on Maharajah Jungle Trek

> Another opportunity to see the astonishing animals of Disney's Animal Kingdom is along the Maharajah Jungle Trek in the Asia area.
>
> See fruit bats, one of the largest species of bat in the world. Komodo dragons and water buffalo are there to greet guests along with birds native to Asia.
>
> The highlight of the Maharajah Jungle Trek comes with the tigers roaming and greeting guests. New to this enclosure are two baby tigers. Watch as they grow up right before your eyes with their mother watching over them.
>
> Do not miss this great chance to visit with animals from Asia in this tree-covered path.

☐ Get soaked on Kali River Rapids

> Board a raft and traverse the treacherous Kali river with your group. These white waters offer a wild

ride through the jungle and be careful of waterfalls that will drench your boat.

Staying dry is not an option on this white-water adventure, so enjoy the scenery and enjoy the cool water on a hot day.

☐ Explore the forbidden mountain and survive the Yeti on Expedition Everest

One of the newer peaks to grace Walt Disney World is the Expedition Everest at Disney's Animal Kingdom.

Get ready for this high-speed chase through the mountain top as you avoid the Yeti. Read about the explorers who barely escaped with their lives attempting to climb this peak.

Board your train and climb to the highest point of this mysterious mountain. You may even find your path blocked by missing train tracks.

Hopefully, you will avoid coming face to face with the infamous Yeti. Keep your head if you have to outrun him on Expedition Everest.

- [ ] Ride Expedition Everest from the front of a runaway train

    For those who want a thrill, ask the cast members to allow you to ride in the front of the train. This offers guests an unobstructed view of this magnificent mountain but also offers a terrifying sight of the yeti as you could become his first snack.

- [ ] Experience the River of Light show after the sun goes down

    The centerpiece of the Asia area is a large body of water where guests can experience River of Light. Become one with the natural world as this show lights up the night sky to show the variety of big and small animals that make up the jungle world.

    Water jets combine with music and fire to dazzle the senses. Get your front-row seat for this wonder of the natural world at Disney's Animal Kingdom.

Dinoland U.S.A.

☐ Find the Olden Gate Bridge at the entrance to Dinoland U.S.A.

As you enter Dinoland U.S.A., you will see an amazing bridge spanning the walkway. The Olden Gate Bridge features a Brachiosaurus standing fifty-two feet high. This fossil greets guests as they start their adventure in Dinoland U.S.A.

☐ Join in the archeology dig at the Bone Yard

Let the little ones run wild as they discover fossils in the Boneyard. Watch as the kids jump, run, and slide through the archeological dig. Fun and learning combine as they can use their skills to find new bones and identify different species.

☐ Read the notices on the bulletin board left by the archeologists

Near the Bone Yard, a large bulletin board stands with dozens of notices from the archeologists and their interns. Find a new car or discover where the staff hangs out at night. Read some of the notices left by the professor or perhaps find a new job.

☐ Try your hand a Fossil Fun Games

Any roadside attraction would not be complete without carnival games to test your skills.

Race your mammoth to the finish line, whack the Packycephalosar or Bronto-score by shooting hoops. Take home a prize for your skills and determination while at this entertaining roadside carnival in Dinoland U.S.A.

☐ Hold on to your hat on Primeval Whirl

Escape a meteor shower as you ride along and snake your way to safety. Not only a rollercoaster, but the Primeval Whirl also combines the thrills of a coaster with the spin adding to your excitement.

Do not miss this thrilling coaster while at the Fossil Fun Games.

☐ Visit Chester and Hester's, one of the roadside shops to see their collection of Dino stuff

No roadside attraction would be complete without a souvenir shop offering travelers an assortment of odds and ends to take home in addition to the shelves lined with Dinoland themed merchandise.

Look high above at the ceiling overflowing with Dinosaur themed posters, toys, and arts and crafts.

Chester and Hester can be found among the shelves in a picture of the founders. Find the rock band miniature or the dinosaur outline using a measuring tape. This out of the way shop is a treasure trove of the tacky and unique in Dinoland U.S.A.

☐ Find the fossil of Sue along the cretaceous path

Walk the Cretaceous path found on your way to DINOSAUR! And you will find the fossil of Sue, the largest and most complete Tyrannosaurus Rex in existence. This fossil has been instrumental in helping archeologists learn about these enormous predators.

☐ Find the red, yellow and white pipes with the chemical formula for Mustard, Mayo, and Ketchup

The level of detail throughout the theme parks at Walt Disney World is amazing, and the queue for DINOSAUR is no exception. Just before the loading area, look up towards the ceiling and find three pipes, one red, one yellow, and one white. The chemical compound found written on these pipes should be familiar to anyone that walks beneath. These are the chemical compounds for ketchup, mustard, and mayonnaise.

☐ Travel back through time to save an Iguanadon on DINOSAUR!

> Enter the Dino Institute and take a tour of a lifetime. Hop in the time rover to go back in time to the Cretaceous period to bring back an Iguanadon before the end of life on earth.
>
> As if a meteor shower is not enough to be concerned about, you will need to escape the powerful jaws of the Carnotaurus as he tries to make you his dinner. Will you get back to the institute in time or will you be left in the time where dinosaurs roamed the earth.

☐ Relive the adventures in the Finding Nemo stage show

> Join Nemo, Marlin, Dory, and all their friends in this live-action stage show retelling the Pixar classic *Finding Nemo*.
>
> Travel with Marlin and Dory as they brave the open ocean to travel to 42 Wallaby Way Sydney. Escape from sharks, jellyfish, and ocean mines before finding Nemo in the clutches of a dentist and his crazy niece.
>
> Become one of the tank gang as they initiate Nemo into the brotherhood of tank hood. Sing along with

Crush as he helps Marlin and Dory through the EAC.

Become part of the action as you clap and sing along to these familiar tunes in the Finding Nemo stage show.

☐ Grab a bite to eat at Restaurantoaurus

Enter the extinct garage and sit down for a meal at this dinosaur-themed eating establishment in Dinoland U.S.A.

From hamburgers to fries, something for every appetite can be found. Look around at the magazine clippings and notices near the ordering area and sit in the garage where the mechanics have left behind dinosaur-themed artwork.

☐ Find the American Crocodile in Dinoland U.S.A.

Throughout Disney's Animal Kingdom, wild animals surround you, and the Dinoland U.S.A. area is no different. If you look around the area near the DINOSAUR attraction, you will find an American Crocodile on display. Most guests think this predator is not real, but be assured, he is as real as the rest of the animals in the theme park.

Disney's Hollywood Studio

Introduction

The third theme park to open at Walt Disney World, Disney Hollywood Studios, opened May 1, 1989, as Disney-MGM Studios with one hundred thirty-five acres of attractions offering guests a behind the scenes look at Hollywood.

The original concept was for there to be a movie-themed pavilion at Epcot, but the idea was expanded to be another complete theme park. On opening day, this new park included a backlot studio tour and the Great Movie Ride as the core attractions with street performers and shops rounding out the opening day attractions.

Within a few years, the park would expand to include the Twilight Zone™ Tower of Terror that would bring guests into the action of their own episode of the classic television show.

By 2004, Disney would include the Lights Motor Action show that debut at Disneyland Paris as a part of the Disneyland 50th anniversary with many attractions being recreated throughout the Disney parks worldwide.

Over the years, Disney-MGM Studios would become Disney's Hollywood Studios as new attractions would draw huge crowds. Aerosmith™ Rockin' Rollercoaster, the Indiana Jones Stunt Spectacular, and Star Tours would bring thrills to guests looking for exciting rides to add to their time at the Walt Disney World theme parks.

Now, Disney Hollywood Studios has created the world of Star Wars with Galaxy's Edge. The definition of thrill rides has been recreated to bring guests an immersive experience into the world of science fiction.

Hollywood Blvd

☐ Visit with the citizens of Hollywood

Enter the gates of Disney's Hollywood Studio and find yourself transported back to the golden age of Hollywood. Walk along the street and see the citizens of Hollywood walking along to greet you.

Get pictures with these adorable characters to remember your time in Hollywood.

☐ Get your picture at the signpost at the entrance of Disney's Hollywood Studios

To the left of the entrance, you will find a multicolored signpost with the names of cities throughout the world. Most guests walk right by without ever noticing this little detail, but this signpost offers a fun and unusual photo opportunity.

Some guests may recognize this signpost as a nod to the classic television show *M*A*S*H** in which the doctors and nurses created a signpost in the center of the camp with the towns where each called home.

- [ ] Visit Adrian and Edith's Head to Toe

    Among the many shops on Hollywood Blvd is a small shop, Adrian and Edith's Head to Toe. While most guests do not give this apt name a second glance, those who know their Hollywood history grin as they step inside.

    Adrian was a well-known costume designer known for designing costumes for *The Wizard of Oz, Pride and Prejudice, The Women, The Philadelphia Story, and Ziegfeld Girl*. Some of the stars Adrian designed for included Judy Garland, Lucille Ball, Norma Shearer, Katharine Hepburn, and Lana Turner.

    Edith Head, also a costume designer, best known for the gowns from *All About Eve, Sabrina, Sweet Charity, and Roman Holiday*. Stars known to wear Edith Head designs included Marylin Monroe, Bette Davis, Audrey Hepburn, and Shirley McClaine.

- [ ] Get your picture taken with Grauman's Chinese Theater in the background

    One of the most iconic facades in Hollywood, Grauman's Chinese Theater, has been the backdrop to every movie star in Hollywood. Opening in 1927, Grauman'sChinese Theater played host to every major movie premier of the golden age of Hollywood. Best known for the forecourt hand and footprints, celebrities clamored for the opportunity to place their hands in wet cement for Sid Grauman.

Today, Disney's Hollywood Studios recreated this iconic building for guests to pose for their photographs. Do not miss this golden opportunity to include yourself in the history of Hollywood at Disney's Hollywood Studios.

☐ Admire the hand and footprints in the forecourt of Grauman's Chinese Theater at Disney's Hollywood Studios

Disney's Hollywood Studios recreated the look and feel of Hollywood, right down to the smallest detail. If you stand in front of Grauman's Chinese Theater and look at the cement in the forecourt, you will find a treasure trove of celebrity signatures around you.

While you will recognize the signature of Mickey Mouse, Donald Duck, and Goofy, you will be pleasantly surprised to find your favorite actors and actresses among them. Mouseketeer Annette Funicello, *Mary Poppins* actor Dick Van Dyke, the voice of the Genie and Comedian Robin Williams, the voice of Mrs. Potts and actress Angela Landsbury are just a few of the famous people immortalized in cement.

Spend some time and find your favorites among the famous at Grauman's Chinese Theater.

☐ Join Mickey Mouse in Mickey and Minnie's Runaway Railway ride

Step into a Mickey Mouse cartoon when you join the famous mouse with his best girl, Minnie, on a picnic that has gone awry. Disney Imagineers have brought cartoons to life as you participate in the fun in the first attraction based on Mickey Mouse himself.

Goofy is your engineer as you travel through the countryside and through town. Survive a cyclone or travel beneath the waves on your exciting adventures.

☐ Dine-in Hollywood style at the Brown Derby

Step back in history to the famous Brown Derby restaurant. As you walk through the doors of this iconic restaurant, you will be met with hundreds of caricatures of your favorite celebrities lining the walls.

Enter the opulent dining room and feast on Brown Derby's signature dishes, cocktails, and desserts.

See and taste what it feels like to be a celebrity as your wait staff treats you like Hollywood royalty during your meal.

Sunset Blvd

- [ ] Ride Rock N' Rollercoaster starring Aerosmith™

    Step through the doors of G Force records just in time to see your favorite Rock group, Aerosmith™, rehearsing for their big concert.

    Just your luck, you are a VIP guest at their concert, but can you get there on time? Yes, when you hop in the super stretch limo and take off through the Hollywood freeways to get there on time.

    Join the high-speed fun with Aerosmith™ supplying the soundtrack to this roller coaster.

- [ ] Visit the Hollywood Tower Hotel and fall into another dimension on Twilight Zone™ Tower of Terror

    Become the star of your own Twilight Zone™ episode as you walk through the doors of the Hollywood Tower Hotel. Leave your reality behind as you join those that have been lost to time.

Tour the lobby that stands still before entering the library to discover the lost souls that disappeared decades before.

Do you dare to test your fate? Climb aboard an elevator and hold on as you may not make it back alive.

☐ Find props from iconic episodes of the Twilight Zone™

For fans of the Twilight Zone television show, now is your chance to come face to face with the props from your favorite episodes.

Look around the library to find the little fortune-telling box from *Nick of Time* starring William Shatner. As you exit your ride through the gift shop, find the telephone from *Long Distance Call* starring Billy Mumy, the talky Tina doll from *Talky Tina* starring Telly Savalas are just a few of the props used in this classic television series.

Spend a little bit of extra time looking around for items from this famous television show.

☐ Revisit a tale as old as time with the Beauty and the Beast stage show

Watch as a tale as old as time comes to life at Disney's Hollywood Studios. Watch Belle, Beast, Lumiere,

Cogsworth, and Mrs. Potts sing and dance for your enjoyment in this outdoor setting.

Sing along to your favorite songs from this classic Disney film. Cheer the hero and boo the villain and cry a little when they live happily ever after.

☐ Watch Mickey Mouse battle the forces of evil in Fantasmic!

Every night, when darkness falls, watch Mickey Mouse battle the forces of evil in the Fantasmic theater.

Mickey battles villains from classic Disney films with the help of his hero friends. Watch as the battle climaxes with fire, water, and forces of both good and evil that will keep you on the edge of your seat.

Make time to see this magnificent performance at Disney's Hollywood Studios.

☐ Explore the Once Upon a Time shop at Carthay Circle

One of the shops on Sunset Blvd has a very special place in Disney history. As you enter the Once Upon a Time shop, you will notice many photos of Walt Disney and celebrities decorating the walls.

These photographs commemorate the opening of *Snow White and the Seven Dwarfs* at the Carthay Circle Theater in Los Angeles.

☐ Explore the Beverly Sunset Boutique

Enter the Beverly Sunset Boutique and find a large selection of Pixar themed merchandise from your favorite films.

Whether you are looking for toys, apparel, or food, the Beverly Sunset Boutique will be your new favorite at Disney Hollywood Studios.

☐ Find the luggage on Sunset Blvd

Guests walking down Sunset Blvd may not even notice the set of matched luggage sitting on the curb waiting for their owners, but there is a fun back story around this odd detail on Sunset Blvd.

If you look closely at the owner tag on the luggage, you will find the name Gilbert London. This is the name of the gentleman you see in the elevator on Twilight Zone Tower of Terror. This ill-fated man left his luggage behind when he disappears from our world.

☐ Visit Lightning McQueen's Racing Academy

Join Lightning McQueen as he shows you how the professionals train for the greatest races. Lightening will demonstrate the latest in training technology, but he needs to be careful, or one of his rivals may take over the race.

Animation Courtyard

- [ ] Visit with Mickey Mouse and all his Disney pals in the Disney Junior Dance Party!

    Join Mickey Mouse and all his friends in this interactive dance party for the kids.

    Doc McStuffinstake time from caring for her pets to celebrate. Vampirina flies in to show off her dance moves, and Timon travels from the jungle to bring his own songs to enjoy.

    Get your dancing shoes on with Mickey Mouse as your little ones celebrate life.

- [ ] Relive the tales of Ariel in the Voyage of the Little Mermaid

    Travel under the sea to relive the story of *The Little Mermaid* in this retelling of the Disney film.

    Join Sebastien as he brings the party to life with his sea creature friends. Fall in love with the story of

Ariel and Prince Eric once more and boo the evil Ursula as she tries to take over the ocean.

Believe in magic as they live happily ever after in this classic fairytale.

☐ Visit with your favorite Star Wars characters at the Launch Bay

Travel to the outer reaches of space as you arrive at Launch Bay. Visit with BB8 as he talks to you and poses for pictures. Get a big hug from your favorite Wookie Chewbacca or join the dark side with Darth Vader and Kylo Ren.

Relive your favorite Star Wars moments as you travel through the Launch Bay area but beware of Storm Troopers on patrol.

☐ See authentic movie props from the Star Wars films

Throughout Launch Bay, guests will find screen-used props from the Star Wars universe of films. From miniatures to costumes, guests can see the movie-making process from behind the camera as you come face to face with your favorite Star Wars films.

☐ Decorate your home with beautiful artwork at the Animation Gallery

> Disney souvenirs do not just include clothing and toys. High-end artwork to adorn your walls is available to guests at the Animation Gallery.
>
> Find the perfect piece of artwork for your home, including oil paints, animation cells, and character sketches. Find adorable sculptures of your favorite characters or scenes from your favorite Disney films.
>
> Do not miss this fantastic opportunity to bring the Disney magic home with a piece from Animation Gallery.

☐ Relive the life of Walt Disney World founder Walt Disney in One Man's Dream, a walk-through museum

> In each theme park throughout Walt Disney World, guests live the vision of one man, Walt Disney. The life of this legendary man can be followed in Walt, One Man's Dream, a walk-through museum dedicated to the life and work that Disney created.
>
> From the humblest beginnings, Disney's drive and passion led him to leave his family home and try to make his dream a reality in Los Angeles. See the successes and failures that created everything guests experience today.

See the path Disney followed to create your favorite Disney characters. Walk alongside Disney as he sat on a bench at Griffith Park and first envisioned Disneyland.

From cartoons to full-length feature films, from theme parks to community outreach, Disney's passion has created a world that has touched the lives of millions of people.

Relive this legendary life in Walt, One Man's Dream.

☐ Watch the life of Walt Disney narrated by Julie Andrews in Walt, One Man's Dream

No trip to Walt Disney World is complete without paying tribute to the life of Walt Disney. Enter the theater and watch the journey of this remarkable man, narrated by none other than Julie Andrews.

Family photos and film bring this man's journey to life once again as you walk in Walt's footsteps.

Make time to pay tribute to the creator of Mickey Mouse on your next trip to Disney's Hollywood Studios.

Toy Story Land

- [ ] Pose for pictures with the bigger than life Woody doll

    From the moment you turn the corner to Toy Story Land, the fun begins as you are greeted by none other than Andy's favorite cowboy doll, Woody. Stop and pose for pictures with this famous cowboy doll. As you bring the fun.

- [ ] Watch the green army men drum corps

    Surprises can come from anywhere in Andy's backyard. Throughout the day, the green army men will come to entertain guests with their precision drum corps. Join in the fun as these adorable toys show off their talents.

- [ ] Walk through Andy's Room in the queue for Toy Story Mania

    Andy's imagination has been busy throughout Toy Story Land. Enter the queue for Toy Story Mania and see how Andy has been busy with his toys and games throughout his room.

Lincoln Logs, Tinker Toys, board games, and card games surround you as you work your way through the queue for Toy Story Mania.

Clay, crayons, and markers create childhood artwork to decorate the walls. Relive childhood memories with your favorite toys and games. A lifetime of memories is waiting for you in Andy's room at Toy Story Mania.

☐ Try your hand at old-fashioned carnival games in Toy Story Mania

Try your luck as you take a crack at games of skill on Toy Story Mania. Andy's games come to life as you shoot darts, throw eggs, hit the targets, and earn points. Play as a team or against the rest of your friends as you rack up the points in four different games of skill.

Look around at the scads of games and toys around you as your car spins. Do not forget to say hello to your favorite Toy Story characters while playing this exciting game.

☐ Take a picture with the bigger than life Buzz Lightyear

Standing high above the Alien Swirling Saucers is the greatest space ranger of all time, Buzz Lightyear. Get this golden opportunity to get a picture with Buzz as he towers over the landscape of Andy's backyard.

☐ Fly through the galaxy on Alien Swirling Saucers

> Find yourself on an alien space ship as your imagination take flight. Swirl through a star-filled galaxy with the tiny minions of Buzz Lightyear as the music sends you soaring to the heights of outer space.

☐ Open Woody's Lunchbox and enjoy lunchtime

> Playtime is not complete without time for lunch. Stop at Woody's Lunchbox and dig in to renew your energy before play continues.

> Sit on a mini Babybel cheese wheel and relax in the sunshine of Andy's backyard. Take notice of the animal crackers Andy has left behind along with wrappers from his favorite snacks.

☐ Find your new favorite toy in Toy Story Land

> Playtime does not have to end when you leave Andy's back yard. Find your new best friend among the many toys available. Whether you like games, stuffed animals, light up swords, or dress up, you will find new ways to stretch your imagination with the toys in Toy Story Land.

☐ Join Slinky Dog Dash for a thrilling roller coaster ride

Hop on the back of Slinky Dog as he flies through the track on Slinky Dog Dash. Andy has been busy at work building track throughout his back yard so that Slinky Dog can race with his favorite friends. Watch as the barrel of monkeys get in on the fast-paced fun.

Finally, enjoy the song stylings of Wheezy as he serenades you with *You've Got a Friend in Me* before your ride is through.

☐ Explore the toy decorations throughout Toy Story Land

Wherever you explore in Andy's backyard, you will find Andy has been using his imagination to use everyday objects and toys to create a whole new world. Find the stacks of checkers, game pieces, pencils, and Christmas lights strung across the walkways and over Slinky Dog Dash. Scrabble tiles used as signage and the toy boxes to decorate the attractions in Toy Story Land.

No matter when you look, you will find something to delight your senses in Toy Story Land.

☐ You're your picture with the Pixar ball

The Pixar ball is an icon of the Pixar films, and now this bigger than life ball has arrived at Andy's backyard waiting for you. Pose for pictures with the Pixar ball next time you wander through Toy Story Land.

Star Wars: Galaxy's Edge

Join the rebel forces as you enter this outpost on the edge of the galaxy. Fly along with your crew on the Millennium Falcon or join the resistance to rise up to fight for your freedom.

Build your lightsaber weapon or your new droid before finding your Jedi robes in the marketplace.

For Jedi's looking for sustenance on their long journey, stop at Docking Bay 7 or pick up blue milk for the long road ahead.

Warning, there are spoilers to the attractions and films within this chapter. Please be aware of this before reading about the areas contains in Star Wars: Galaxy's Edge.

☐ Walk through the tunnel to Batuu

   Galaxy's Edge cannot be seen from any other area in Disney's Hollywood Studios, so walking through the tunnel to Batuu can make guests feel like they have arrived on a remote outpost.

As you walk down the path and through the tunnel, the world of Batuu comes alive before your eyes. The Imagineers have created a way to bring guests the thrill of experiencing this land as if they were landing on a far distant outpost of space.

Now it is time for you to experience Batuu for yourself.

☐ Get your picture taken in front of the First Order TIE Echelon

This twin ion engine shuttle is the perfect backdrop for your pictures while on Batuu. Be sure to stop and get photos in front of this impressive First Order transport before it takes off for another mission.

☐ Read the signs around Batuu

Aurebesh is the official language of Batuu, and those visiting will notice that most of the signs around this outpost are written in this language.

While the alphabet of Batuu is not posted anywhere on the outpost, guests can download the Disney app and translate the signage to translate these signs and store names into your language.

☐ Learn the phrases spoken on Batuu

The citizens of Batuu will greet travelers with phrases that may not be recognizable to guests visiting for the first time. But you will get to know the greetings very quickly.

Learning these phrases is very simple, but some are secret codes to ensure that the First Order does not discover your allegiance.

Ignite the spark – this is a resistance greeting

Light the fire – the response to Ignite the spark

In no time, you will be a native speaking with the citizens of Batuu.

☐ Try the blue or green milk

Any fans of the Star Wars films remember when Luke Skywalker walked into the cantina, and they caught their first glimpse of the blue milk. Many years later, we watched Luke drink green milk after milking the female Latha-Siren.

Now guests of Batuu can sample these for themselves at the outdoor vending area.

- [ ] Enjoy a beverage at Oga's Cantina

    Travelers can stop for a refreshing beverage at Oga's Cantina, a cantina similar to Mos Eisley Cantina, as seen in *Star Wars: A New Hope*.

    Now travelers can step up to the bar or sit in a secluded table to enjoy a variety of alcoholic and non-alcoholic beverages served throughout the day on Batuu.

- [ ] Enjoy the music of D.J. R-3X

    While in Oga's Cantina, you will listen to the sounds of D.J. R-3X, and this little droid should look familiar to anyone who has visited Star Tours over the years. This droid is Rex, the pilot of the Starspeeder 3000. Rex has been retired from his service with Star Tours and now has a new purpose at Oga's Cantina.

- [ ] Watch as the hyperdrive malfunctions during your time at Oga's Cantina

    Every so often, the hyperdrive that powers Oga's Cantina will stop working. The lights dim, and the music will stop until the staff can get the hyperdrive working once more.

☐ Find the Ewok spear beer tap

> If you look behind the bar at Oga's, you will find a familiar Ewok spearhead with the Yub Nub beer. Fans of *Star Wars: Return of the Jedi* will recognize this beer name is also the song the Ewok's sing in this classic film.

☐ Find Ponda Baba's arm behind the bar at Oga's Cantina

> Fans of *Star Wars: A New Hope* will remember when Luke Skywalker was saved from Pondo Baba by Obi-Wan Kenobi in the cantina. Now guests can find a drawing of his arm on one of the jars behind the bar of Oga's Cantina.

☐ Get your picture with the Millennium Falcon

> The focal point of the Black Spire outpost is the Millennium Falcon docked on this outpost. Guests can now get their picture with this infamous smuggler ship during their time on Batuu.
>
> Be sure to get this perfect memory of your time on this outpost with a picture with the Millennium Falcon.

☐ Find the Sabacc game in the queue for Millennium Falcon: Smugglers Run

> As guests enter the queue for the Millennium Falcon: Smugglers Run, you will notice an area

directly behind the falcon with a small hexagon-shaped table. Notice the cards sitting atop this table are the exact cards used when Han Solo won the Falcon from Lando Calrissian in the film *Solo*.

☐ Find the small red droid from *Star Wars: A New Hope*

In the storage area behind the Millennium Falcon, you will find a small red droid in front of two orange jumpsuits. Guests may recognize this droid as one the Jawas were trying to sell in the *Star Wars: A New Hope*.

☐ Find the Scout Trooper helmet used as a drip pan in the maintenance area

Hidden in the shadows just before guests make a turn to the second level, you will find a scout troopers helmet seen in *Star Wars: Return of the Jedi*.

The resistance has a sense of humor when they repurpose these items.

☐ Watch the sub-light engine come to life on the second level gantry

As guests make their way to the second level, you will see a huge sub-light engine being worked on. Periodically, you will see and hear this engine come to life with lights and sound showing guests that this outpost is actively working.

- [ ] Find Porg nests around the queue area

    As you work your way through the queue towards the lounge of the Millennium Falcon, look around and see if you can find small nests hidden in corners. These are Porg nests waiting for their small inhabitants to return from exploring Batuu.

- [ ] Enter the lounge of the Millennium Falcon

    Enter the lounge and guests will feel like they have just stepped into their favorite Star Wars films. Feel free to sit at the holochess table, but be sure to let the Wookie win.

    Once in a while, guests will hear and see the Falcon power down, be sure to run to the left corner and hit the large red button just in time to bring the Falcon back to life.

- [ ] Find the Marksman-H combat remote

    If you spend any amount of time in the lounge area, you may recognize the helmet used by Luke Skywalker when he trains in *Star Wars: The Empire Strikes Back.* Leaning against this helmet is the small combat droid that Luke was attempting to block in this famous film.

☐ Join the crew of the Millennium Falcon: Smuggler Run

Board the Millennium Falcon and help intercept the Coaxium to gain a healthy profit for your crew and Hondo Ohnaka. Jump to light speed and find the train with your cargo waiting for you to take it for yourself.

But be careful to dodge obstacles and avoid getting caught. Once you reach the base, find out what percentage your crew will earn, less any damages, of course.

☐ Find the frozen Rathtar as you exit the Millennium Falcon: Smugglers Run

As you exit your ride on the Millennium Falcon, look at the walls around you. On one wall you will find a Rathtar frozen in carbonite for all eternity. You may recall the Rathtar chasing Han Solo and Chewy in *Star Wars: The Force Awakens* as they narrowly escape with their lives.

☐ Find the cargo ship above Docking Bay 7 Food and Cargo

High above the entrance to Docking Bay 7 Food and Cargo, you will find a cargo ship that has landed on the outpost. As you look at this ship, notice the numbers 77, 80 and 83. These numbers signify the years that the first three Star Wars films were released.

☐ Stop in at Docking Bay 7 Food and Cargo for a great meal

For those looking for a great meal on Batuu, stop at Docking Bay 7 during your travels. Try the Kaadu ribs with a blueberry corn muffin and a cold Phattro to quench your thirst. Try the Endorian Tip Yip salad or Chilled noodle salad. Be sure to get the Batuu-bon for dessert to top off a delicious meal.

☐ Examine the trash receptacle number throughout Star Wars: Galaxy's Edge

Throughout this outpost, guests will find trash and recycle cans for their garbage. On the trash cans, notice the descriptive writing with the number 3263827. This sign reads, "trash to sector 3263827". For Star Wars fans, this is the very same area where Luke Skywalker, Han Solo, Chewy, and Princess Leia find themselves trapped and being slowly crushed in *Star Wars: A New Hope*.

☐ Explore Ronto Roasters and see who is cooking

Guests getting a snack at Ronto Roasters will find a familiar droid cooking meat. This tall droid was torturing his smaller counterparts in *Star Wars:*

Return of the Jedi when C3PO and R2D2 are given to Jabba the Hut.

☐ Find the sizeable podracer engine cooking the meat at Ronto Roasters

The enormous blue engine is instantly recognizable to Star Wars fans. This podracer engine is cooking the meat turning on the spit at Ronto Roasters so travelers can get a hot meal.

Fans of *Star Wars: The Phantom Menace* remember a young Anakin Skywalker winning the podrace. This engine came off of one of the podracers that was destroyed during a podrace and repurposed to serve hot food daily at the Black Spire Outpost.

☐ Taste the Outpost popcorn mix

Near Ronto's, you will find Kat Saka's Kettle, where they offer sweet and spicy popcorn for weary travelers. The red and purple give travelers a tasty treat to take with them as they explore the shopping stalls.

For those looking for something sweeter, try the chocolate popcorn.

☐ Find you Jedi attire at Black Spire Outfitters

Whether you want to dress like Rey or your favorite Sith, Black Spire outfitters offer everything a Jedi needs to be ready for battle. From shirts to vests to arm wraps to robes, these high-quality clothing items are just perfect for the traveler exploring the Black Spire Outpost.

Be warned, travelers over the age of fourteen will not be able to don their new robes while at the theme parks. Little travelers will be permitted to dress as long as robes do not drag the ground.

☐ Visit Toydarian Toy Maker

Zabaka, the toymaker, has been working hard making toys for travelers visiting the Black Spire Outpost. Stop in to find plush toys and puzzles to keep you entertained during your long travels through Batuu.

If you look above, you will find many tributes to your favorite Star Wars moments. Above the cash register area, guests will find Darth Vader and Obi-Wan Kenobi locked in a battle to the death. Nearby, the Millennium Falcon is racing through space chased by the empire, and Jabba, the Hutt's sailing barge, sits high on one of the shelves.

Be sure to watch the silhouette of Zabaka through the frosted glass busy at work on his next creation before you continue through the stalls.

☐ Find Watto from *Star Wars: The Phantom Menace*

Just outside Toydarian Toy Maker, you will see a sign with a small green creature. Fans of *Star Wars: The Phantom Menace* will recognize Watto, the owner of Shmi and Anakin Skywalker.

☐ Visit Creature Stall for your new pet

Find adorable creatures from all over the galaxy at the Creature Stall on Batuu. For some travelers, the Wampa is their creature of choice; for others, the cuddly loth cat is more their choice.

Be sure to look through all the creatures up for adoption but do not miss the creatures in the high cages. If you look closely at the cages with the tags, you may see glowing eyes staring at you from the depths of their cage. Ask the proprietor about adopting today.

☐ Find Han Solo's landspeeder from the film *Solo*

As you explore the stalls in the market, you will come across a small rack with three landspeeders. The blue speeder on the bottom once belonged to Han Solo in the film *Solo*. Be sure to get a picture of this miniature version of this famous landspeeder.

☐ Visit the Droid Depot for your new mechanical friend

This small shop offers guests a once in a lifetime experience. Step up to the conveyor belt and pick the parts of your droid as they roll by you. Once you have selected the perfect pieces, take them to the assembly area, and you now have your working droid to take home. Once you have your new friend, he will be placed in a handy carrying vessel to make transporting this little droid easier.

☐ Find the imperial enforcer droid from *Rouge 1* within the Droid Depot

Within the many cages in Droid Depot, you will find one containing a large grey headless droid. Some may recognize this as K-2SO from the film *Rouge 1*.

☐ Find the remains of the Imperial probe droid outside the Droid Depot

As you exit the Droid Depot, look at the junk area in the rear. Hanging in this area is an Imperial Probe Droid that has seen better days. Fans may recognize this as the droid that was looking for the rebels in *Star Wars: The Empire Strikes Back.* Since then, this droid has been seen in various incarnations of the Star Wars universe.

- [ ] Explore the collection within Dok-Ondar's Den of Antiquities

    Travelers from every galaxy come to Dok-Ondar's Den of Antiquities to find treasures only seen on the movie screens. Masks, collectibles, lightsabers, and Kyber Crystals are just a few of the choices available within this shop. As you wander through this shop, Busts of your favorite Jedi or Sith can be purchased. Kyber Crystals will glow for you when you configure them correctly or Jedi gear, including patches for your robes.

- [ ] Find the golden head of Jar JarBinks among the upper-level collection

    Among the vast number of items on the second level, a golden head of Jar JarBinks can be found atop a box waiting for the perfect travelers to take home.

- [ ] Admire the Medal of Bravery at Dok-Ondar's

    High above, hanging on the wall behind the main counter, you will find the very medal presented to Luke Skywalker and Han Solo in *Star Wars: A New Hope*. Get a picture of this fantastic medal before your time in Dok-Ondar's is complete.

☐ Marvel at the taxidermy animals in Dok-Ondar's

Several exotic animal heads can be found within Dok-Ondar's. Guests may recognize the Tauntaun and the Nexu from the Star Wars universe among the various creatures displayed.

☐ Find the taxidermy Wampa on the second level of Dok-Ondar's

The large white animal standing on the second level is very intimidating, but do not be afraid. This Wampa is the very creature that attacked Luke Skywalker on the frozen planet of Hoth in *Star Wars: The Empire Strikes Back,* and now he is on display for travelers looking for the very unique.

☐ Create your own lightsaber within Savi's Workshop

Join in this ancient Jedi ritual of building your own lightsaber within Savi's workshop. This secretive ceremony offers travelers a chance to create their custom lightsabers complete with the activation ceremony.

Once your ceremony is done, slide your new weapon in the custom sleeve to carry with you as you explore the rest of the outpost.

☐ Find the landspeeder from *Star Wars: A New Hope*

In a far end of the Black Spire Outpost, you will find a garage with several vehicles waiting for maintenance. One of these vehicles is familiar to fans of *Star Wars: A New Hope*. The landspeeder Luke Skywalker and Obi-Wan Kenobi travel in when the travel to Mos Eisley Spaceport.

☐ Interact with the Stormtroopers as they interrogate travelers

As you wander through Batuu, be on the lookout for Stormtroopers interrogating guests. These stormtroopers are looking for a member of the resistance Vi Moradi, and you may even see them chasing this elusive member of the resistance through the streets of Batuu.

Stay on your best behavior, or they may detain you for questioning.

☐ Watch out for Kylo Ren looking for members of the resistance

The infamous Kylo Ren is personally looking for members of the resistance throughout the First Order encampment. You may find the son of Han Solo near Docking Bay 7 with his Stormtroopers keeping him safe.

Be sure to avoid interrogation as he may detain you if he suspects you know something about the resistance.

☐ Find Chewbacca around the resistance base towards the mountain outpost

Chewbacca can be found nearby the Rise of the Resistance to pose for pictures and interact with travelers looking to join the resistance. The loveable Wookie loves posing with guests while he wanders through the back roads of the Black Spire Outpost.

☐ Interact with Rey around the Rise of the Resistance area

Rey is traveling the back roads nearby Rise of the Resistance, posing for pictures and signing autographs with travelers. Be sure to stop if you happen to see this new generation of Jedi warrior during your travels through Batuu.

☐ Watch Chewbacca and the resistance fixing the X-wing fighter near Rise of the Resistance

Travelers navigating the road around Rise of the Resistance may find Chewbacca and several members of the resistance trying to fix one of the X-wing fighters in the evenings. Be sure to take some time to watch them argue and work on this fighter during your time in Batuu.

☐ Ride Rise of the Resistance

The resistance is looking for new members, and it is your turn to join them to assist in defeating the First Order.

Traverse the hidden passageways within the mountain and travel to the secret base. Be careful, so you do not become prisoners on a Star Destroyer. If you find yourself the prisoner of the First Order, cooperate and do not give away the secrets of the rebels.

Echo Lake

☐ Take part in the retelling of Frozen in For the First Time in Forever: A Frozen Sing-Along Celebration

Relive the story of Anna and Elsa in this retelling of Frozen. Join in on all the songs from your favorite Disney film when the storytellers of Arendelle bring the story to life once again.

Sing along to *Let it Go* and *For the First Time in Forever* as the cast of Frozen takes to the stage. Before you know it, Queen Elsa will bring her special magic to the theater when she makes it snow in Orlando, Florida.

Do not miss this opportunity to relive this new Disney classic in For the First Time in Forever: A Frozen Sing-Along.

☐ Meet Olaf at the Celebrity Spotlight

Everyone's favorite snowman is waiting to meet you at Disney's Hollywood Studios. Olaf is ready to take pictures and interact with guests in this exclusive meet and greet right next door to the Frozen theater.

☐ Discover the hints from *Who Framed Roger Rabbit* in the buildings around Echo Lake

Guests walk through Disney's Hollywood Studios but rarely look around at the detail all around them. Spend some time around Echo Lake and find the billboard advertising Maroon Cartoons with several of your favorite Characters from *Who Framed Roger Rabbit* staring down at you.

Across from this billboard, find the offices of Eddie Valiant, the detective hired to spy on Jessica Rabbit, and the window broken in the shape of Roger Rabbit. These are just some of the fun Imagineers had creating the area.

☐ Stop for a cocktail at the Tune-In Lounge

Celebrate the invention of the television while cooling off with a cocktail at Tune-In Lounge. This lounge brings back the feel of the 1950s when television was brand new, and the shows became instant classics.

Order your favorite drinks from the talented bartenders while indulging yourself in your favorite television shows at Tune-In Lounge.

☐ Indulge in comfort food at the 50's Prime Time Café

Step through the door of 50's Prime Time Café and step back in time. Experience a meal like your grandparents and great grandparents ate while exploring the furnishings of the 1950s.

As you wait for your table, watch black and white television or read some of the book titles along the bookshelves. Sit at the Formica table while you enjoy your meal. Just be sure to finish your vegetables, or you might get a surprise at the end of the meal.

☐ Watch the nail-biting adventures in the Indiana Jones Stunt Spectacular

Join renowned archeologist Indiana Jones and his adventures in this live-action show that jumped right off the silver screen. Join Dr. Jones as he explores the temple ruins, saves the heroine from the enemy and the grand finale before escaping in the nick of time.

Do not miss this live-action show on your next trip to Disney's Hollywood Studios.

☐ Volunteer as an extra for the Indiana Jones Stunt Spectacular

Be selected by the casting director and see the show from right in front of the actors. Get into your costume and join your fellow actors as you shop in the Bazaar and watch as Indiana Jones and Marian fight off the bad guys and flee from their clutches.

- [ ] Tug on the rope of the archeology dig and listen for the archeologist to ask you to stop before a priceless artifact goes crashing down

    Just outside the Indiana Jones Stunt Spectacular, you will find a well in the middle of the archeological dig. The archeologists are hard at work beneath the surface finding priceless artifacts to bring to the museum.

    If you tug the rope, you may hear them telling you to stop or even hear the crash of a priceless vase.

- [ ] Watch the younglings defeat Darth Vader and complete their Jedi training in Jedi Training, Trials of the Temple

    Sign your little ones up for Jedi training at Disney's Hollywood Studios, and they can join the force when they study with a Jedi master.

    Their final exam will be to defeat Darth Vader on the training stage near Star Tours. Be sure to sign them up early to ensure they get their spot for this elite training experience. At the end of their training, each Jedi will receive a certificate to commemorate their time at the Temple.

☐ Watch the flight information screen in the Star Tours queue

As you enter the building for Star Tours, the large screen will show advertisements, weather and flight information for the various galaxies that Star Tours flies to. Be sure to read the flight information on gates, take-off times, and weather on the planet you plan to spend time visiting.

☐ Watch C3PO and R2D2 get the Starspeeder3000 ready for take-off

As you work your way through Star Tours' main queue, you will see C3PO and R2D2 getting a Starspeeder ready for the next flight. These two droids argue and interact with the guests as they work on their projects.

☐ Watch the droid scan luggage for contraband

As you enter the shipping area of Star Tours, stop for a few moments to see the luggage go through the scanner. You may recognize some familiar items within the suitcases as you listen to the luggage scanning droid give its commentary on each item it sees.

☐ Save the rebel spy and escape Darth Vader in Star Tours the Adventure Continues

Enter your Starspeeder 3000 and get ready for a trip of a lifetime.

Save the rebel spy from Darth Vader as you travel across the galaxy. Jump through hyperspace to race through the ice of Hoth, the forest of Kashyyk, or Tatooine to escape capture.

Get your boarding pass for Star Tours today.

Commissary Lane

- [ ] Dine at the Sci-Fi Dine-In Theater restaurant

    Arrive on set and get into your convertible to enjoy a meal while watching classic Science Fiction movie trailers and commercials. Laugh along with the silly exploit of these 1950's movies as you enjoy classic burgers and do not forget the shake to top off your dining experience.

- [ ] Stop at the ABC Commissary

    For those looking for a hearty meal during their day at Disney's Hollywood Studios, stop at the ABC Commissary. Select from many mouth-watering selections and ice-cold drinks.

    Be sure to stop at the Lucite boxes along the main entrance to see props and costumes from your favorite ABC television shows.

☐ Meet the iconic Mickey and Minnie Mouse

Walk the red carpet with Mickey and Minnie Mouse as they greet guests daily at Disney's Hollywood Studios guests.

Minnie is ready for a red-carpet event in her glamorous couture gown, and Mickey has his Sorcerer's Apprentice robe for great pictures.

Grand Avenue

☐ Visit Muppets courtyard and see how the Muppets have made it their own

The Muppets have made their mark on Grand Avenue, and guests visiting this area of Disney's Hollywood Studios will see firsthand how they have recreated this area.

Whether it is the fountain featuring Miss Piggy or the funny signage throughout Grand Avenue, no matter where you look, the Muppets have found a way to make this area their own.

☐ Find the key under the mat at Muppet Vision 3D

As you enter the building for Muppet Vision 3D, the first area you will pass by is security, but the security does not seem to be very secure. If you lift the mat in front of security, the key to the building is under the mat waiting for security to return.

☐ Read the signboard for Muppet Vision 3D headquarters

As you enter the building for Muppet Vision 3D, you will pass by a signboard with the directory for the various departments. Be sure to take a moment to read the signboard and laugh at the hilarious divisions of Muppet Studios.

☐ Find the net full of Jello™ inside Muppet Vision 3D

Before entering the theater for the demonstration, you will enter a pre-show area with hundreds of props and costumes strewn around the room. High above your head, you will notice a net full of blocks. This is the famous net full of Jello™.

Why would they include this unusual prop in Muppet Vision 3D? This is a tribute to the most famous Mouseketeer, Annette Funicello.

☐ Enjoy the Muppet Vision 3D attraction

Join Kermit, Piggy, Fozzie, and all their friends as they demonstrate the Muppet Vision 3D technology. Enjoy songs, dances, and comedy as the Muppets try their best to keep the show from going wrong.

Be sure to get your seat for the next showing of Muppet Vision 3D.

☐ Find the multi-colored pipes behind Muppet Vision 3D

Guests walking through the Grand Avenue area will find many hilarious details, but most guests walk right by the multi-colored pipes without ever wondering what the pipes could mean to the Muppet universe.

These pipes are a nod to the Muppet artists. In 1964, Jim Henson, Frank Oz, and several other Muppet artists were scheduled to appear on the Jack Paar show in New York's NBC studios. The group of men got bored backstage and found a utility closet with many colors of paint and used this paint to create their artwork on the building pipes on the floor of the building.

Not only did NBC save the pipes from being painted over or removed during renovations, but the pipes are now part of the NBC tour. They have been preserved behind glass to remain forever as a memorial to this famous story.

☐ Find the paint splatter outside the exit to Muppet Vision 3D

One of the Muppets has been busy painting the building bright yellow but did not finish the work before slipping and spilling the paint down the building and onto the concrete below.

☐ Enter the Stage 1 Company Store and read the hilarious signs

Enter the Stage 1 Company Store, and you will find yourself backstage at Muppet Studios. Inside you will find props and scenery along with various signs warning guests and actors.

Find the five laws of show biz or the chickens only beyond this point to see who else is not permitted.

Be sure to spend some time inside the Studio 1 Company store.

☐ Find the sets from *The Great Muppet Caper*

Within the Studio 1 Company Store, guests will find a quiet corner with a second floor with rooms. This area is directly out of the film *The Great Muppet Caper,* where Kermit Fozzie and Gonzo stay at the Happiness Hotel.

☐ Dine at PizzaRizzo's

Rizzo the Rat has been busy opening his own pizza place at the Grand Avenue, and now you can have a slice of pizza and a cold drink.

Walk around and see some of the record albums and street signs inside the restaurant before heading upstairs to eat in the ballroom ready for your next great event.

☐ Grab a bite at Mama Melrose Ristorante Italiano

Guests looking for a great Italian meal can eat at Mama Melrose Ristorante Italiano at the Grand Avenue. Get your reservations for your next vacation in this authentically decorated restaurant.

☐ Find the tomato loading zone near Mama Melrose

Outside Mama Melrose, you will find a large sign for the tomato loading zone. If you look very carefully, you will notice the sign is covered in tomatoes that have been thrown at the sign and doorway.

Holidays at Walt Disney World

Halloween

Magic Kingdom

☐ Enjoy the Halloween décor throughout the Magic Kingdom

The Magic Kingdom is bustling with décor for the Halloween season. Jack-O-Lanterns and scarecrows are decorating Main Street U.S.A. while wreaths and garland in Yellow Orange and red decorate every inch of the theme parks.

☐ Visit the candy store for special Holiday treats

Throughout Halloween, guests can find sweet Halloween themed treats. Find the bright orange Halloween cupcake, or the Mickey-shaped cinnamon roll will give guests a flavor of this fun Halloween.

For guests looking for something fresh, stop at the ice cream shop for a scoop of pumpkin ice cream.

- [ ] Find Halloween themed merchandise throughout the Magic Kingdom

    Every Halloween, guests will find dozens of new Halloween themed merchandise to take home as a souvenir of your time during the Halloween season. Whether it is T-shirts, plush toys, plastic pumpkins, or headbands, guests will find the perfect souvenir of Halloweentime at the Magic Kingdom.

- [ ] Ride the Pirates of the Caribbean during Halloween

    During Halloween, the Pirates of the Caribbean holds surprises for guests who dare travel these haunted waters. Join the pirates as you spy the cursed treasure to travel to the time of Pirates but beware of some new faces that may just be talking directly to you.

- [ ] Join the Monsters at Monster's Inc. Laugh Floor for Halloween

    The monsters have been busy writing new Halloween themed jokes for the Monster's Inc. Laugh Floor to tickle your funny bone. Be sure to join the audience to hear the latest giggle-worthy jokes.

- [ ] Go to the Mickey's Not So Scary Halloween

    Join Mickey Mouse and all his friends as they celebrate Halloween at the Magic Kingdom. Don your costume and go trick or treating throughout the theme park. Watch as the Disney villains try to take over the park with the help of the witches from Salem. Halloween fun is around every corner during this nighttime Halloween event.

☐ See the Halloween fireworks display at the Magic Kingdom

The Not So Spooky Fireworks at Magic Kingdom top off a magical event with these dazzling fireworks dancing in the sky. Listen to your favorite Disney villains and songs blends to bring the Halloween event to life.

Disney's Hollywood Studios

☐ Dine with Minnie and her friends at Hollywood and Vine

Minnie Mouse and her friends have gotten their Halloween costumes on and are waiting for you at Hollywood and Vine. Grab a fantastic meal and get ready for the fun with pictures and autographs from your favorite characters. Make reservations for this fun-filled event.

Christmas

Magic Kingdom

☐ Enjoy the decoration at the Magic Kingdom

Enter the Magic Kingdom as you join in the fun with holiday décor throughout the theme park. Whether it is the garland, wreaths, or a Christmas tree towering over Main Street U.S.A., you can not help but find the Christmas spirit during your time at the Magic Kingdom.

☐ Find Holiday treats for Christmas

Guests will find fantastic holiday treats throughout the Magic Kingdom during Christmas. Hand decorated apples, Christmas cookie milkshakes, cherry pistachio floats, or the Santa Mickey waffle sundae are just a few of the mouth-watering delights you will find during the holiday season. Come armed with your appetite when you arrive at the Magic Kingdom during the Christmastime festivities.

☐ Attend the Mickey's Very Merry Christmas Party

> Guests will find a magical way to celebrate at the Magic Kingdom during Christmas when they attend the Mickey's Very Merry Christmas Party. See your favorite characters, enjoy Christmas themed shows and fireworks while riding your favorite rides. This once in a lifetime event cannot be missed.

☐ Find a new Christmas souvenir

> The Magic Kingdom has everything for your Christmas list during the holiday season. Whether you are looking for spirit jerseys, headbands, plush toys, or T-shirts, the Magic Kingdom has everything you can imagine for the holiday season.

Epcot

☐ Join the Epcot International Festival of the Holidays

Throughout the World Showcase, guests will find holiday traditions from the eleven countries represented. Stop at each country to try holiday foods, see traditional costumes, and try libations that will make you want to include in your next holiday party.

☐ Attend the candlelight processional

Cast members from the Walt Disney World resort come together to sing for the guests of Epcot each year. See your favorite celebrities narrate this heartwarming event. Be sure to reserve your place for this holiday tradition at Epcot.

Disney Animal Kingdom

☐ See the Tree of Life Awakening's

   During the holiday season, the Tree of Life brings a wintery tale to life as guests see their favorite animals come to life with new holiday music.

☐ See the life-size sculpture puppets

   Talented cast members walk among the guests as they bring these life-size marionette puppets to life. See Reindeer, arctic fox, polar bears, and musicians stroll through the walkways to bring the holiday magic alive.

☐ See the holiday décor throughout Disney Animal Kingdom

   Each area of Disney Animal Kingdom comes alive with the Christmas spirit during the Christmas season. Whether you are in Africa, Asia, or Pandora, guests will find something new to bring the joy of the holidays to life.

Disney's Hollywood Studios

☐ See Jingle Ball Jingle BAM!

Watch as the Hollywood Tower Hotel comes to life each evening during Jingle Ball Jingle BAM! Guests will see the holidays come to life with this spectacular show of lights and entertainment. Be sure to visit Disney's Hollywood Studios for this amazing show.

☐ See the holiday décor at Disney's Hollywood Studios

Hollywood during Christmas is quite a spectacle, and Disney's Hollywood Studios is no exception. See the décor on Hollywood Blvd or Sunset. See how Andy has decorated his back yard for Christmas or visit the Christmas tree on Echo Lake.

Wherever you go, Christmas is in full swing at Disney's Hollywood Studios.

In conclusion, I hope you have enjoyed seeing the Walt Disney World resort with *One Hundred Things to do at Walt Disney World Before you Die*. It has been my great pleasure writing this book, and I hope you have found something that has added to your enjoyment during your time in the theme parks.

I look forward to too many years of the Walt Disney World resort growing and changing. These theme parks have been a part of my life since I was a small child, and I look forward to many more.

www.ingramcontent.com/pod-product-compliance
Lightning Source LLC
Chambersburg PA
CBHW070122110526
44587CB00017BA/2918